THE·CARIBBEAN
"MAKING·OUR·OWN·CHOICES"

NEIL MacDONALD

D1796377

AN·OXFAM·REPORT

Published February 1990
© Oxfam 1990

British Library Cataloguing in Publication Data

MacDonald, Neil, *1950 -*
    The Caribbean: 'making our own choices'
    1. Caribbean region. Social conditions
    I. Title
    909'.09821

    ISBN 0 85598 086 9

Front Cover painting by unknown Haitian artist.
Reproduced by kind permission of Frank Judd.

Back Cover photo by Philip Wolmuth.

Published by Oxfam, 274 Banbury Road, Oxford OX2 7DZ.
Printed by Tekprint Limited.

CONTENTS

Oxfam in the Caribbean	v
The Caribbean at a glance	vi
1. Birth of the modern Caribbean	1
Discovery or desecration?	1
Victory over slavery	2
Sovereignty	4
2. Land, poverty and barriers to development	5
Bananas – a fragile lifeline	6
Haiti – the fate of peasant agriculture	8
Migration: the Caribbean diaspora	14
3. Community organization: in search of solutions	17
"People becoming conscious together"	
– the animation movement in Haiti	17
Community organization in the ghetto	20
Working for health	21
4. Women in the Caribbean	23
Fighting the double burden	24
5. Culture of resistance	29
Keeping alive the hopes of the poor	29
Theatre in education	32
The contradictory Caribbean identity	35
Creole – the politics of language	36
Voudou – the politics of religion	38
Rastafarianism	40
The fight to preserve culture – animation through art	41
6. Disasters – resourcefulness and cooperation	45
7. Conclusion	47
8. What you can do	49
9. A potted history	51
Index	55

THE CARIBBEAN: MAKING OUR OWN CHOICES

OXFAM IN THE CARIBBEAN

You may be surprised to know that Oxfam works in the Caribbean. Or perhaps you already know something of our work from the TV and newspaper reports of the relief effort after Hurricane Gilbert devastated Jamaica, Haiti and the Dominican Republic in 1988.

However, this book is not primarily about relief work, which is only one small part of what Oxfam does in the region. It is about development. That is to say it is about how communities of people work together to create a few more choices, to gain a little bit more control over their lives. It is a book, not about Oxfam, but about Caribbean people, their efforts and their work. It is about projects created and run by Caribbean people, which Oxfam supports. These projects and the people who run them – our project partners – are a source of hope and inspiration to their communities.

We have tried throughout this book to let our partners, past and present, tell their own stories. We hope that their energy and pride will provide hope and inspiration to people here.

Oxfam maintains a regional headquarters in the Dominican Republic, spending just under a million pounds a year in support of Caribbean projects. Other staff in Haiti and Jamaica help to keep us closely in touch with people's needs. The priority is given to Haiti, where need is greatest – it is not just the poorest country in the Caribbean, but also the poorest in the Americas. But poverty is not the only factor in deciding where to give support: support also goes to other communities where people are also trying to shape their own destinies. The neighbouring Dominican Republic and nearby Jamaica also receive significant attention. In the eastern Caribbean, Oxfam works mainly in the Windward Islands: Dominica, St Lucia, St Vincent and Grenada. Plans are underway to start work in Guyana in the near future. Oxfam hopes to help build links between groups in the Caribbean and the communities of Caribbean people who have dispersed to the UK and around the world.

CUBA

JAMAICA

HAITI

DOMINICAN REPUBLIC

THE CARIBBEAN AT A GLANCE

	POPULATION (millions)	AREA (miles²)	GNP ($m)	GNPpc ($)	LIFE EXPECT'CY	LITERACY	MAIN EXPORTS
BARBADOS	0.254	430	1358.90	5350	75	99^	sugar
CUBA	10.2	115000			75		sugar, nickel, tobacco
DOMINICA	0.080	750	115.20	1440	74	80*	bananas, coconut products
DOMINICAN REPUBLIC	6.7	49000	4891.00	730	66	85^	sugar, coffee, cocoa
GRENADA	0.100	345	134.00	1340	69	98*	bananas, nutmeg
GUYANA	0.797	215000	310.83	390	66	91^	bauxite, sugar, rice
HAITI	6.1	28000	2196.00	360	55	37^	coffee, sugar
JAMAICA	2.4	11000	2256.00	940	74	73^	alumina/bauxite
ST LUCIA	0.142	616	198.80	1400	70	80*	bananas, cocoa
ST VINCENT	0.120	388	120.00	1000	69	80*	bananas, arrowroot
SURINAM	0.420	163000	953.40	2270	67	80^	bauxite, oil
TRINIDAD & TOBAGO	1.2	5000	6552.00	5460	70	97^	oil

Source: World Development Report 1989, World Bank
* = from Green Gold, Latin America Bureau
^ = from InterAmerican Development Bank 1987
pc = per capita

THE CARIBBEAN: MAKING OUR OWN CHOICES

BIRTH OF THE MODERN CARIBBEAN

t was a clear October day in 1492 in the islands that would later be called the Bahamas. The Caribbean waters sparkled a translucent blue in the sun. The air was clear and fresh. Brightly coloured humming birds whirred through the wooded shoreline and the scarlet hibiscus flowers. The Amerindian islanders were busy, as usual, fishing the deep waters offshore as well as the foreshores and reefs from canoes made from logs. Inland, they farmed the crops their ancestors had brought from the mainland of South America: cocoa and corn, sweet potatoes and arrowroot, pineapple and citrus fruits, beans and peanuts, guava and papaya, cotton and tobacco. These still form most of the crops that are produced today in the islands. But their world was about to end forever. On that day they discovered Christopher Columbus, washed to their shores by the Atlantic currents and still thinking he had discovered a new route to India. He was impressed by the gentleness of the islanders.

> *"Believe it Your Highness that in the whole world there cannot be a better nor gentler folk ... of singular ways, loving and sweet-tongued."*
>
> **Christopher Columbus to the King of Spain, 24 December 1492**

DISCOVERY OR DESECRATION?

Their way of life didn't long survive the arrival of the European colonists. Within a century the Tainu, the peaceable Arawaks and the fierce Caribs were all but exterminated. Only a few isolated groups of Caribs still survive today in the small islands of the eastern Caribbean. The Arawaks are still remembered in Jamaica's coat of arms. The Tainu bequeathed to us the words 'hammock' and 'maize'.

Toussaint L'ouverture?

VICTORY OVER SLAVERY

The Caribbean is often described as a 'melting pot' of cultures, peoples and races. But the fires that produced that melting have been, at times, fierce and painful: flames of war and conquest; of slavery and exploitation; of racial hatred and rebellion. They were the fires of the furnaces on the great sugar plantations, where slaves seized in chains from West Africa toiled in the fields to cut the cane, and in the mills to crush and boil off the sugar. The Haitian nation, the first black republic in the world, was born in 1804 in the flames of a slave uprising led by the slave Toussaint 'L'Ouverture' against the French colonists, and a 13-year civil war.

The Haitian slave rebellion sounded the death knell for slavery throughout the Caribbean. In England manufacturing was replacing trade as the engine of wealth. The new captains of industry, above all, wanted

EGBERT WATKINS, SMALL FARMER, JAMAICA

"Sometimes you ate roots so hard on your jaws you couldn't speak."

Egbert Watkins, president of the Hillside Farmers' Association, scratches his greying beard with the handle of his cutlass as he remembers the struggle that made farmers of cane cutters. *"The government said 'land to the landless'. But the big men wanted the land."*

The Hillside Farmers' Association is made up of 54 families of poor farmers. The land where they grow cane, sweet potatoes, corn and fruit is sandwiched between the bauxite plant of Clarendon Alumina Productions Ltd and the Monymusk refinery of the Clarendon Sugar Company – symbols of Jamaica's natural wealth past and present. The Hillside farmers come from the Jamaica that has not grown rich on this wealth. They were granted 740 acres on a 49-year lease in 1975 through a government land programme. But the land did not come easily to these families who had been cane cutters on the sugar estate.

"The big men at Monymusk wanted it and we fought them bitterly. When they found we had the land they shut off the [irrigation] water. We sweated blood. We ate poor. Sometimes you ate roots so hard on your jaws you couldn't speak. We negotiated for 10 years. At first they gave us a little water. We went back day after day to the Monymusk office. We didn't just go once. We went until they said 'not them again! give them what they want!'. Sometimes they used words I couldn't understand what they said. But we kept going back. From that time we were getting water."

The deal they struck with the Monymusk estate guarantees them water to irrigate their crops so long as they grow some sugar cane for the estate. They only break-even on this at best, but it keeps the water flowing and relations with the estate calm. Asked if they would go back to cutting cane on the plantation, one farmer replied *"Our own cane, yes. Our own cane. But back to the estate? There's nobody of us here that is willing to go back."*

Monymusk Estates, owned at that time by the Tate and Lyle company, was not the only multinational company that regretted tangling with the Hillside Farmers. The trains carrying alumina from the bauxite refinery to the west passes across HFA land, and the alumina dust thrown off the wagons began to corrode the galvanized iron roof of the HFA office and meeting house. The refinery was owned at that time by the US multinational, Alcoa. *"We went to the Alcoa office and said 'what recompense you going give us?'"* remembers Egbert. Again, persistence won. The company finally agreed to re-roof the office, and to help them dig a small dam to retain irrigation water.

The Hillside Farmers are proud of what they have achieved. In 1975 they were an anonymous group of poverty-stricken cane cutters, living, like many rural Jamaicans, scattered across the estate. Today they have laid the foundations of a hard-working community of farmers, and are moving towards setting themselves up as a cooperative. Oxfam helped them, through the local agency Projects for People.

The history of the Caribbean, like the history of the Hillside Farmers, is inextricably linked with sugar. The archipelago's sugar plantations were the rich prizes over which Europe squabbled: the Spanish conquerors, the Dutch, English and French colonists and the North American companies who followed them in the scramble. This history of war and conquest is seen very differently in the Caribbean than it is in Europe. Francis Drake, for example, is honoured in Britain as Elizabethan swashbuckler and hero of the defence against the Spanish Armada; in the Caribbean he is remembered as a pirate and plunderer.

cheap food for their workers. They did not want the expense of protecting (militarily as well as economically) the 'inefficient' plantation agriculture of the Caribbean. The advocates of free trade found common cause with reformers. Slavery was abolished in the English colonies in 1833 and in the French in 1848. Later still in parts of the Caribbean, after the slaves, came Asian labourers, recruited in the near-slavery condition of 'indenture' (tied labour contracts) from India and China to fill the labour deficit on the plantations. The abolition of slavery happened piecemeal in the ex-Spanish colonies: 1822 in the Dominican Republic, 1873 in Puerto Rico and 1880 in Cuba.

SOVEREIGNTY

The sense of community is strong in the friendly, small and intimate societies of the Caribbean. But it is an identity forged against the background of strong pressure from outside.

Political independence has been hard-won and economic sovereignty remains elusive. The Commonwealth Caribbean became independent from Britain only after 1962. Guadeloupe and Martinique remain French territories, while Holland still owns the four islands of the Netherlands Antilles. And, even for those territories which became independent in the last century, the nearby United States has been a powerful, and at times overbearing, neighbour.

Between 1915 and 1934, Haiti was run by the US marines as was the Dominican Republic between 1916

and 1924. Even in the post-war period, US troops have been in operation in the Dominican Republic (1965) and Grenada (1983).

Cuba and Puerto Rico which won their freedom from Spain only in the course of the Spanish-American war of 1898-1901, then passed into the effective control of the US. Puerto Rico remains closely associated with the US with the status of an *"Associated Free State"*. This status, which prompted the United Nations Decolonization Committee to call (14 August 1985) for the self determination and independence of the island, is due to be re-examined in a forthcoming plebiscite.

> "During [the early decades of the twentieth century] I spent most of my time being a high-class muscle man for Big Business, for Wall Street and, for the bankers. In short, I was a racketeer for capitalism. ... thus I helped make Mexico and especially Tampico safe for American oil interests in 1914. I helped make Haiti and Cuba a decent place for the National City Bank to collect revenues in... I helped purify Nicaragua for the international banking house of Brown Brothers in 1909-1912. I brought light to the Dominican Republic for American sugar interests in 1916. I helped make Honduras 'right' for American fruit companies in 1903."
> **Gen. Smedley D. Butler, Marine Corps commander, Caribbean Basin**

LAND, POVERTY AND BARRIERS TO DEVELOPMENT

2

The Caribbean's struggle to nationhood since 1804 has been dominated by the fact that the islands originally entered the world economy, not as independent communities, but as plantation colonies. Sugar was sown in the seventeenth century to serve the rapidly expanding European market for this new luxury commodity. This set the pattern for Caribbean development as single-crop economies. And it also created a sharp social divide between the rich, white, elite of planters and the poor, black, mass of slaves. The heritage of that divide still bedevils the Caribbean.

The region today remains dependent on commodities whose prices it does not control. Sugar is still a major export, though declining in importance. The banana industry, which developed in Jamaica and the eastern Caribbean in the nineteenth century, produces another major export. In the twentieth century, the discovery of bauxite (from which aluminium is made) in Jamaica, Guyana (previously British Guiana) and Surinam (previously Dutch Guiana), as well as oil and asphalt in Trinidad, have provided additional sources of income. Yet poor people have seen few of the benefits.

This year we goin' in celebration
Freedom from bondage and oppression.
A hundred and fifty years of emancipation.
To celebrate is to be misled.
Because my people are still underfed.
Night-soil men are still carrying the filth instead.
And Antiguans are still carting water on dey head.

The Truth

"Banana is killing us, not only financially but socially."

BANANAS –
A FRAGILE LIFELINE

In the Windward islands everything is centred around the banana trade which is in the hands of a foreign fruit company. The islands' economic life centres on the visit of the banana boat every fortnight. In Dominica, for example, where bananas make up 60% of exports, the Banana Grower's Association sell all the bananas to the British shipping firm Geest who provide credit facilities and access to fertilisers and pesticides.

Currently a special trading relationship between Britain and its former Caribbean colonies means that there is a guaranteed market for the crop produced in these islands. In 1992 the introduction of the single European Market may mean the end of the special trading agreement and the Windward Islands will face stiff competition from other countries where bananas can be produced much more cheaply.

This is one reason why Windward islanders are beginning to rethink their dependence on bananas. Earlene Horne, the good-humoured, bantering, and incredibly hard working General Secretary of the National Farmers' Union in St Vincent, says there are environmental reasons too: *"Banana is killing us, not only financially but socially.*

"If you add it all up it's just not profitable. Banana need a lot of land – the more you grow it the more you need so farmers are cutting down the forests to produce more. Bananas have brought us a range of chemicals over the years

PHILIP WOLMUTH

that are killing us. The plastic used to cover the banana to protect them, do not rot easy and there's no way of getting rid of it. In our rivers there used to be fish but they've all gone, not just because the amount of plastic that has been washed into them, but bananas are often grown on slopes near rivers and streams and chemicals sprayed onto the crop run into the water.

"They tell us overhead aerial spraying is harmless but we're beginning to see a number of our birds disappearing. If we weigh it all up we realise banana is doing us a lot of harm."

A third reason for trying to end this dependence is the vulnerability of the banana crop to storm damage. It takes little more than a high wind to knock down the almost rootless banana tree.

Clement Nation is a Dominican farmer who has already taken the decision to diversify his farming. He is in his thirties, with nine children (six of whom live with him and work on the farm) and five grandchildren. Hurricane Hugo hardly left a mark on his farm. Although he grows six acres of bananas to sell – most of which he lost – Clement also grows pineapple, passion fruit, mangoes, oranges, limes, coconuts, and the root crops dasheen and yam, as well as breeding rabbits, chickens, pigs, hens and goats. The electricity which powers

> *"In our rivers there used to be fish but they've all gone ..."*

In September 1989, Hurricane Hugo, which, wreaked damage in the dependent territories of Puerto Rico, Guadeloupe and Montserrat, destroyed 70% of Dominica's banana crop.

his home is supplied by Biogas – alternative technology, which Oxfam helped to provide, that transforms manure into gas – so nothing is wasted!

Some farmers in St Vincent are also beginning to grow different crops. But, without alternative markets, it is a difficult decision to make. Earlene Horne explains:

"We have discussed this problem of a one-crop economy. But we have to face reality. We have an established market for bananas. We can grow a lot of things here. For example, ginger. It grows here and hurricanes don't damage it. We could be the biggest producer of ginger around. But the problem is the market. The market for ginger is sometimes there and sometimes not. The same with yams, sweet potatoes. Hurricanes don't damage them. Our members are calling on the union to do something about marketing for non-banana crops."

She feels that 1992 should be looked on as the perfect opportunity to get rid of the reliance on bananas once and for all. The St Vincent National Farmers Union has been talking to farmers, government ministers and grower's associations to look at ways of finding new markets and to look at how countries like Britain can help set up new markets in a less dependent context.

HAITI: THE FATE OF PEASANT FARMING

Attempts to build a base for economic development have stressed export-earnings. In most cases this has favoured the big companies. Small-scale agriculture on which many poor

IN SEARCH OF A ROUTE TO DEVELOPMENT

DEVELOPMENT – WHO BENEFITS?

Agricultural exports

Though some territories have managed to diversify, sugar, and in the eastern Caribbean bananas, remain the main source of export earnings for many Caribbean countries. Sugar accounted for 51% in Dominica, 49% in Guyana, 9.5% in Jamaica and 1.7% in Trinidad in 1982. But world prices for sugar have remained depressed since the late 1970s. Uncertainty about access for rum and bananas to the European market under the European Community's Common Agricultural Policy has made the situation worse, especially with the impending creation of the single European market in 1992.

Minerals

The bauxite in Jamaica, Guyana and Surinam and the oil and asphalt in Trinidad have not solved the development problem. They created isolated high-tech enclaves in which foreign companies retained the whip hand. By 1925, the linked north American aluminium companies Alcan and Alcoa had secured virtually total control over the bauxite deposits in Guyana and Surinam. In 1977 Jamaica and Guyana together supplied 65% of the US's bauxite imports, with Haiti, Surinam and the Dominican Republic supplying a further 25%. The foreign companies kept most of the profits while the poor received few of the benefits. The bauxite industry is capital-intensive and provides few jobs. The US$300m invested in Jamaica by the bauxite companies between 1950 and 1970 created only about 6,000 permanent jobs. Tax revenues due to the governments were systematically undervalued by

the companies. Most of the smelting of the relatively cheap crude ore into high-value aluminium was done abroad. So while most of the value was added outside the Caribbean, the environment was pocked with the pollution of red mud lakes.

Tourism

In more recent years, tourism has become, for many, the main alternative source of hard currency earnings. Tourism started early in Jamaica, in the 1960s when rich Americans abandoned Cuba as their playground after Fidel Castro's 1959 revolution. The industry has become the main source of hard currency for Jamaica, with tourist spending more than doubling between 1979 and 1985 to over US$400m. Other territories, with fewer natural resources than Jamaica,

PHILIP WOLMUTH

have become even more dependent: almost half of the labour force in the Bahamas, and almost a quarter in Antigua-Barbuda are employed in tourism. The Dominican Republic is making an energetic bid for a greater share of the market, with tourist income more than doubling between 1979 and 1985 to just under US$300m. Here again foreign, particularly US, investment was dominant. Over half the hotel capacity in Jamaica and Barbados is in foreign hands. And much tourist spending remains in the North (payment to tour operators etc), thus reducing the benefits to the Caribbean. Tourism is also notoriously volatile, depending on climate, fashion, economic conditions in the US and the fluctuating cost of air travel. A bad season can have a devastating effect on a small economy. Furthermore its social effect is to create a luxury enclave, predominantly white, in a background of poverty, predominantly black.

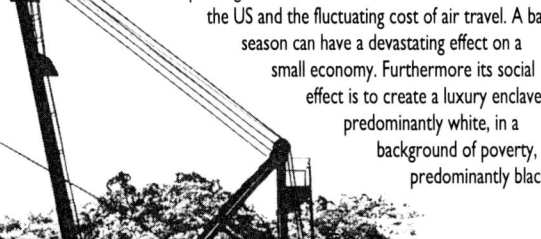

families depend has languished.

Haiti illustrates starkly what has happened to peasant agriculture. A gulf grew after independence between the countryside and the town, between the black peasants and the mulatto elite who formed the commercial, governing and professional strata. The two became almost separate nations – in colour, in language, in religion, in economic and social relations. The black peasants spoke Creole, practised voudou, farmed increasingly small and subdivided parcels of land, and practised common law marriage or often polygamy. The elite spoke French, worshipped in Catholic churches, did no manual work, and practiced legal, monogamous marriage.

Pressure on the soil increased after the French left in 1804. Some of the land remained in the form of big sugar estates. But some was divided between the ex-slaves. Their descendants have become more and more crowded onto smaller and smaller subdivided plots. Not surprisingly, yields have fallen dramatically. Farmers cling, eking out a meagre living, to the most astonishingly inhospitable spots. Throughout the mountainsides that cover much of the country, lean goats and cows graze at crazy angles on the slopes. So steep are the hillsides that farmers tilling their plots of maize, sorghum, beans, sugar cane and citrus fruit are tilted as if they were leaning into a strong wind. Drought is frequent. High taxes, land rents and grasping middlemen further squeeze the pitifully tiny incomes of the farmers.

Nothing illustrates the precarious plight of the Haitian farmer so much as the saga of the creole pig. Haiti's pig population was wiped out between 1978 and 1982, after a massive outbreak of swine fever and the slaughter of the surviving animals. For poor peasants, many of whom had already lost their land, this was the last straw: their pigs were the only source of income they had to meet emergencies such as illness, deaths or debts. The government responded by importing new breeding pigs from the United States. But American pigs were very different beasts from Haitian pigs. The creole pig was adapted to Haiti: it ate scraps, it walked itself long distances to

PHILIP WOLMUTH

INDUSTRIALIZATION AND THE NEGLECT OF AGRICULTURE

The model of development based on industrialization, export-oriented agriculture and enclave production, was intended to improve export earnings. In fact, it has had the reverse effect, by increasing balance of payments problems. Food imports have become a significant necessity – food in 1982 represented around 10% of total imports in Trinidad and Tobago, 8% in Guyana, 16% in Jamaica and 28% in Grenada . There are other 'knock-on' effects. In Jamaica, for example, bauxite production aggravated an already serious land shortage as mining companies bought up over 100,000 acres of land from peasant farmers. Agriculture languished and more and more people drifted to the cities in search of work.

Many Caribbean governments have established 'Free Trade Zones' to attract foreign investment and soak up a growing urban labour force. The lure to the foreign companies is low wages and tax holidays. The Dominican Republic heads the league table with no fewer than 19 free trade zones and a further 11 under construction. The garment and 'assembly' industries which have set up shop, however, create few jobs. In Jamaica, for example, the 1960s was a decade of industrial growth, but this growth was paralleled by rising unemployment – from 13% in 1960 to 26% by 1968.

THE CARIBBEAN: MAKING OUR OWN CHOICES

2

JOSE RODRIGUEZ, COFFEE FARMER, DOMINICAN REPUBLIC

José Rodriguez sits perched on a sack of coffee beans. He leans forward earnestly as he explains:

"We work from seven in the morning to five in the afternoon. But coffee doesn't bring the farmer much profit. The benefits of the coffee go to the middlemen. They cheat on the value of the product. Then there are the taxes. All they leave the small farmer is his work, his human sacrifice and that of his family. We, the small coffee-growers, produce the national wealth, but where we are, we have nothing which permits us to live like human beings. We don't have medical centres, schools, roads, bridges, much less a chemist's or a doctor. And as for food, it is at pauper's level, even though we produce the wealth. Of every 100 pesos, we are losing the benefit of around 46. But here [at the cooperative] it's different. Here the benefits go to the farmer, not to enlarge the capital of the merchant."

José is a member of the Nucleus of Coffee Farmers' Associations of Baní – a market town in the south of the Dominican Republic. He is taking his turn working for a year as warehouseman in the Nucleus, leaving his wife and brother to tend the family plot in the hills. The small coffee producers have begun to pool their resources in order to reap more of the benefits of what they sow. They are by-passing the big exporters who control the coffee trade (the country's second biggest export crop), and trying to do their own marketing.

In the first year in 1976/77, small farmers across the nation made a start by capturing over one and a half per cent of the export trade. By 1988, they had almost a 10% slice of the market. Over 98% of coffee in the Dominican Republic is produced by small farmers. In many other parts of the Americas, coffee is grown on big estates. But in the Dominican Republic, about 69,000 small growers work plots of less than six hectares (about 15 acres). Coffee was first planted in the eighteenth century by run-away slaves who had escaped to the remote and inaccessible mountains. Most plots yield less than 4,000 lbs of coffee a year – about one-twelfth of what they could produce with more investment. Here too is where the benefits of banding together come in, providing credit for investment and channels for technical training. The small coffee producers began to get together after Hurricane David in 1979 destroyed much of the coffee crop.

They have formed into local associations, and the associations have joined together into Nuclei. The Nuclei, in turn, have come together in a Federation. The Baní Nucleus serves around 900 members. It offers warehousing, processing and cheap credit. For José this is a step towards making real his dreams of electricity, proper schooling for his children, and health care for the whole family.

> *"Small coffee-growers produce the national wealth, but we have nothing which permits us to live like human beings."*

market, it was tough and resistant. It's distant northern cousin is a pampered animal, fussy about its food, unwilling to walk large distances and lacking in resistance to Haitian conditions. Expensive to keep and difficult to adapt, the imported pigs were ill-suited to the peasants' needs. The government at first refused to allow import of creole pigs from Jamaica and Martinique. Later in selected areas throughout the country, organizations like the National Association of Haitian Agronomists were able to help groups of farmers establish a breeding stock of creole pigs and give them training in husbandry so that they could avoid a new outbreak of disease. This work is continuing.

THE ENVIRONMENTAL THREAT

Two hours northwest of Port-au-Prince, eroded mountains thrust up from the fertile rice plain like stripped giant carcasses – bare ribs of white rock jutting through the tattered remains of greenery. The rivers run brown with more topsoil washed away in the last rains. Beyond the rice plain, cactus and scrub take over, harbingers of the desert that threatens to engulf the northwest in ecological disaster.

Once this whole island, that the French colonists used to call the "*pearl of the Antilles*", was heavily wooded. Then the trees were cut, the rare woods like mahogany for export and the rest for firewood and for house-building, leaving the fragile soil exposed to wind and rain.

There have been some attempts at reforestation. Further to the south, along the coast at St Jean du Sud, the church-based group Haitian Christian Community Development (DCCH) is promoting conservation. In an area of 200 hectares, on which 600 families are dependent, training sessions and the establishment of tree nurseries are helping to contain erosion.

PHILIP WOLMUTH

GROWING EXPECTATIONS AND THE SEARCH FOR ALTERNATIVES

Responses to frustrated expectations of development have been most dramatic in the larger states. In the 1970s nationalist governments in Guyana, and then Jamaica tried to take on the power of the bauxite multinationals. The Guyanese government of Forbes Burnham in 1971, began a programme of nationalization of key foreign-owned enterprises that brought 80% of the economy into state hands. Pressure by the multinationals and the US government eventually won agreement from Forbes Burnham to pay compensation at higher than the book value of the expropriated enterprises. Jamaica, under the People's National Party government of Michael Manley, in 1974 took a 51% share of the bauxite industry. But the PNP policy of 'democratic socialism', announced in late 1974, frightened investors. Capital began to flow out of the country. Though Manley was re-elected in 1976, the economy rapidly worsened. He lost power in the 1980 polls to Edward Seaga's conservative Jamaica Labour Party, amidst scenes of unprecedented violence between supporters of the two rival parties. Seaga's tenure, which was renewed unopposed in 1983 when the PNP boycotted that year's election, was characterized by economic recession which showed some signs of lifting in 1987, until the devastation of Hurricane Gilbert in 1988 delivered a hammer-blow to the island's hopes. Support for Seaga declined as the state of the economy worsened and social services deteriorated. Manley was returned to power in the 1989 elections, and his administration has been characterized by fence-mending with the US and international financial institutions.

But the economies of the smaller islands of the eastern Caribbean are even more vulnerable. Largely dependent on sugar and/or bananas, with attempts of varying degrees of success to develop a tourist industry, the basic viability of some is in question. Unemployment runs as high as 25-30%. Growing discontent among the poor is a social powderkeg.

The powderkeg exploded in Grenada in 1979. A bloodless coup by Maurice Bishop's New Jewel Movement overthrew the conservative government of Eric Gairy. The NJM government's policy was one of non-alignment internationally and promotion of a mixed economy at home. The conservative governments of the eastern Caribbean islands were alarmed and feared the spread of 'communism'. In a characteristically self-fulfilling prophecy, Grenada's requests for aid were turned down by most traditional donors, pushing the country towards the eastern bloc. In 1983 Bishop was murdered in a bitter faction fight within the NJM. This murder afforded an opportunity for the Organization of Eastern Caribbean States to invite in US military forces. After a week of fighting the US troops gained control of the island and put in a caretaker government.

PHILIP WOLMUTH

MIGRATION: THE CARIBBEAN DIASPORA

Family budgets in many territories have been hit hard in recent years. Falling prices for export commodities, the national debt burdens and austerity policies undertaken by governments have translated into unemployment, low wages and reduced social services. For many families trapped in this situation, a hidden support comes from the money sent home by family members living and working abroad. As economic problems have mounted, increasing numbers of people have left the Caribbean. After the Second World War, Britain urgently needed workers in the new national health service, in industry and in the public system, and thousands of people from the English-speaking Caribbean answered the call. As the social and economic climate in Britain became less welcoming, the United States became an increasing magnet. Today one person in five of Caribbean origin lives permanently in the United States. The Caribbean peoples have become a world-wide diaspora. The dollars and pounds sent back to the Caribbean are a vital part of the survival strategies of many families.

THE HULTON-DEUTSCH COLLECTION

DEBT AND THE BALANCE OF PAYMENTS CRISIS

In the 1980s Caribbean countries have faced mounting debt problems and have been forced to trim social spending in line with the 'austerity' measures – known as structural adjustment – prescribed by the international lending institutions as the cure for economic ills. These institutions like the International Monetary Fund usually demand that governments cut budgets for public services like health and welfare before they will agree to further loans.

A noted Caribbean economist, Richard Bernal of the Jamaican Workers' Bank told Oxfam in 1987:

"What we have in the Caribbean is a lot of people. We don't have much else. And development is about people. Therefore cutting ... services puts in question the basis of development. When you had this level of unemployment in Europe you called it the Great Depression. But we live with these levels of unemployment permanently.

The prevailing international financial institutions (the World Bank and the International Monetary Fund) were set up to safeguard the world economy. But what is good for world trade is not necessarily good for a Third World country. They assume that adjustment means restoring the efficient functioning of the economic system, but it is the structure which is creating the deficits. For example, maintaining primary product economies which keep producing more physically but earning less from it. The diagnosis is that the problem is misallocation of resources, whereas there is also the problem of resource creation. The problem is not whether you can get shoes $1 cheaper, but whether you can put people to work... The International Monetary Fund asks for deregulation of wages so that supply and demand can come into equilibrium. Of course supply and demand can come into equilibrium, but will it be at the level of a liveable wage? I don't think so.

What we need is structural transformation, not structural adjustment. There must be a recognition that balance of payments adjustment must be socially and politically viable -otherwise social upheaval undermines the adjustment process. It must stress import substitution as well as export promotion, and it must respect economic sovereignty. The International Monetary Fund and The World Bank are service organizations. Nobody set them up as policemen. People forget that they are United Nations organizations. They have managed to sever that connection. But they are responsible to the UN. They must respect our economic sovereignty and not ram their programmes down our throats."

"When you had this level of unemploy- ment in Europe you called it the Great Depression."

BELINDA COOTE

TABLE 1

TOTAL EXTERNAL DEBT (PUBLIC AND PRIVATE) OF SELECTED CARIBBEAN COUNTRIES (1987)

	Debt (US$m)	Debt per person (US$)	Debt as % of GNP	Debt service as % of exports
DOMINICAN REPUBLIC	3071	458	66.3	21.7 (1986)
HAITI	674	110	30.2	7.0
JAMAICA	3569	1487	141.2	27.5
TRINIDAD & TOBAGO	1635	1363	39.3	13.2 (1986)

Source: World Development Report 1989, World Bank

COMMUNITY ORGANIZATION: IN SEARCH OF SOLUTIONS

3

The organization of coffee growers in the Dominican Republic, described in the last chapter, illustrates an important general lesson that Caribbean people have been learning about development: that if they want change in their lives, they need to rely on themselves and their communities. Solutions emerge when people get together.

"PEOPLE BECOMING CONSCIOUS TOGETHER" – THE ANIMATION MOVEMENT IN HAITI

Father Yvon Joseph is a priest, a small man with a big laugh. But he becomes deadly serious when he talks about the poverty in Haiti. He says:

"*In Europe and the United States, people are suddenly talking about unemployment. Here, nobody talks about unemployment because there is no employment. We have had this bad situation where people have to depend on others for their food [international food aid]. There is a house I used to go and visit where they had put up a sign saying 'Bread and more than bread'. People don't want to receive their bread from others. They want the conditions for earning their own bread. So, it's 'bread and more than bread'. To understand these conditions – why people don't have bread, don't have work, don't have schools or clinics – that is what takes time. That's the main starting point for our work.*"

Father Yvon works for IDEA (Diocesan Adult Education Institute), a Haitian organization that trains local communities in the north of the country to understand and deal with their problems. The aim is not so much to provide technical solutions as to help people find their own solutions. This is what Haitians call "animation". Father Yvon calls it "people becoming conscious together". This is at the core of the development process in Haiti.

Solutions emerge when people get together.

A good example of this process is provided by the work of another organization: the Development Research Group (GRD), working in the south of the country. A member of GRD's staff explained:

"It is easy to give aid and money. But you have to ask whether that solves the problem. A person may come and ask for money today, and again tomorrow, and again the next day. But the problem isn't solved. With education, people start to ask for other things. People have to want to improve their lives so that they are not dependent on handouts. For example we helped the landless farmers here [in the southeast] to start a tool bank. Many landless people don't have tools. And if they work on someone's land without tools, using the landlord's tools, their

wages are cut in half. At first we ran the tool bank. Within two years the tools had all disappeared. People borrowed them and never returned them. Now, instead, there is an association of landless labourers. They run the tool bank themselves, not us. It is their tool bank. Now, no tools are stolen."

Father Yvon agrees that solutions, if they are to work, must come from the people themselves:

"For years the agronomists had been saying that people should store part of their grain, build silos to hold it immediately after the harvest when prices are at the their lowest and sell it later when prices rose again. There was no response. Then we started a small credit scheme to help people improve their marketing. As they increased the volume of their trade, they themselves came up with the need for storage silos."

"You see", he chuckled, *"out of a small programme which had nothing to do with silos came the suggestion of silos."*

At the heart of this development process are small mutual-aid groups – the animation groups. Starting in the 1970s, Haitian peasant farmers began to pool their resources in small groups to try and find modest ways to improve their standard of living. Some groups worked a common plot of land to supplement their diet and incomes. Others worked together on irrigation projects. And educational centres like IDEA, Papaye and ITEKA, as well as support organizations like GRD, began to grow up, to provide technical advice and training.

It is the training that makes the difference between piece-meal aid and development. Animators, people from the communities trained by the

PROBLÈM DAYITI

Chimen Pèp-la

Fòk nou konprann ki jan peyi-a ap mache

NAP REDI, MEN FÒ NOU KONNEN POUKISA

PWOGRAM FÒMASYON SITWAYEN KRETYEN – EGLIZ METODIS DAYITI

centres, help communities to think through their needs, to identify the forces that constrain their possibilities, and to widen their options for longer-term development. This description by an Oxfam visitor of the work of an animation trainer gives an idea of the technique:

"*It was amazing how he encouraged the participants to use their own knowledge to make some sense of what they know and see and hear. They discussed the value of development in the form of roads, dispensaries, churches, schools and how all these things, because of the system of graft, work to marginalize the peasant even further. He used an analogy of a bottle with a stopper – controlled by those in power. The majority of Haitians are in the bottle – poor, hungry, in misery. Under the bottle is a fire which makes life in the bottle just awful, pressure laden – this is the lure of watches, fridges, urban life etc. And then there is a valve, representing things like football, clairin (cheap rum), voudou, drugs, which lets out the steam just sometimes. Life seems sometimes confusing in the bottle because just sometimes it seems as though things get better, sometimes the president comes and the road is done and the school is painted. There is even sometimes extra food to be given out. At other times justice is particularly arbitrary and for little reason one is in trouble.*"

Jerôme is a community educator, and animator. He says that "*without education all is destined to perish*". He was originally a small farmer, renting a narrow strip of infertile land in the central plateau of Haiti. A few years back, he got together with 12 neighbours to form a mutual-aid

HAITI – A TOUGH STRONG PEOPLE

In Port-au-Prince, capital of Haiti, people are everywhere in the streets: shuffling, scuffling, scraping for a living. Life is hard. Shoe-shine boys, boys selling cartons of contraband American cigarettes, women selling vegetables from the countryside, children begging, men with rough wooden barrows selling ices made by shavings off an ice block flavoured with syrups of suspiciously brilliant colour poured out of used coke bottles. The brightly painted little buses known as 'tap-taps' bulge with passengers as they race perilously through the bustling streets. Life is hard. And yet there is a pride. People walk tall and straight, almost dancing as they move. This is a tough, strong people. This is the people that freed itself by force of arms from Napoleon's armies in 1804 and almost succeeded in uniting the whole island of Hispaniola after forays across the border into Spanish Santo Domingo. This is the people which provided a source of inspiration for Simon Bolivar and the Latin American freedom movement. This is the people that overthrew the sinister dynasty of the Duvaliers in 1986.

And yet this myth of the warrior people is a contradictory one. A nation proud of its fight against France, whose leaders look to French culture as a model of civilization. A nation proud of its African heritage, where the mulatto elite wears its lighter skin like a badge of office. A nation that cherished its independence and its national liberation struggle throughout the nineteenth century, only to be militarily occupied by US marines from 1915 to 1934. Yet, even then, Haiti did not surrender its independence easily. Charlemagne Péralte led the first guerrilla war faced by a US army of occupation – several years before the better-known guerrilla war led by Sandino against US troops in Nicaragua. Tragically, this, the first black nation to win its freedom from colonial powers, has also become the poorest nation in the Americas. The average Haitian earns less than £200 per year. And most Haitians are not average – they earn much less. A landless labourer earns around one US dollar a day (about 60p).

DAVID WINDER

PHILIP WOLMUTH

Almost three people in four are unemployed.

group to improve a common plot of land. They found that there were other groups organized similarly. Gradually, the groups began to come together for larger projects. Through the animation groups, poor farmers have gained confidence and greater control over their lives. For example in Jerôme's community they had a discussion about the taxes they are forced to pay when they take their goods to market. They decided they would stop paying them until the authorities gave them services in return, such as shelter from the rain. They carefully worked out in advance how they were going to make their protest, by using role plays to understand what the reactions of the authorities would be. Jerôme explains: *"When people are organized it is not so easy for those who live off them to get rich"*.

Though there is still a long way to go, the Haitian peasants are finally finding their voice. For so long confined to the margins of society, they are now building a movement which can reflect and represent their interests.

COMMUNITY ORGANISATION IN THE GHETTO

With things so difficult in the countryside, more and more people are leaving the land, throughout the Caribbean, and crowding into the cities hoping for a better life. In the poor areas of Jamaica's capital, Kingston, urban deprivation and violence are the symptoms of years of neglect and the current economic crisis. Examples don't come much starker than Hannah Town, a community of 10,000 people. Housing conditions are appalling: most families live in a single room in what is known as a *"yard"*, sharing toilet facilities with others. Women form 80% of the workforce and many are heads of families. Almost three people in four are unemployed. Crime is for many the only means of surviving, and conflicts between rival youth gangs is a growing problem. There is political violence too, with clashes between rival supporters of the two main political parties, especially at election times. People have looked to patronage from local politicians for help. Many see their situation as hopeless.

"Even for people from Jamaica who come here to see the ghetto, it is an experience," says Ralph Hoyte of Hannah Town's United Church. *"You couldn't believe how de-motivated people can become. Not able to participate in your own future and make your own decisions. That's why the process of human development is so critical and so difficult."*

Ralph in 1978 helped to establish and was the coordinator of the Mel Nathan Institute, an attempt to give the people of Hannah Town a say in their future. The Institute runs a primary school, a community college for vocational training, and various income-generating workshops – in shoe-making, basket-weaving, carpentry and food-production. The Institute's work was badly hit by Hurricane Gilbert, which devastated much of Kingston in 1988. Oxfam, which has supported the MNI since 1980 is helping to get its work re-established.

WORKING FOR HEALTH

Casa Abierta (literally, "*Open House*") in the Dominican Republic is another example. Bouncing and jolting your way across the potholed roadways of the capital, Santo Domingo, your car ducks and weaves between the streams of traffic that seem to be in a constant state of rush-hour. You screech to a halt at a traffic light. Immediately the roadway is full of children. One starts to wash your windscreen with a rag from a plastic bucket of dirty water. Another is selling newspapers. A third holds out one hand and, with the other, eloquently rubs the part of his grubby tee-shirt that conceals his belly, gazing into the car with imploring brown eyes. These are the street kids of Santo Domingo. The small amounts of money they bring in can make the difference between eating and not eating for their whole families. They are around at all hours of the day or night. Fun for them may mean hanging around petrol stations,

getting high on gasoline fumes, or sharing a plastic bag of glue.

"*We find boys of eight years old or less who are using glue and gasoline,*" says Casilda Ramos of the drug project Casa Abierta, "*especially the street kids who hang around and sleep in the streets. Or kids whose parents have to leave them in the home all day.*"

The street kids' solvent abuse is by no means the only or the major drug problem in the Dominican Republic, which is increasingly being used by the Colombian drug mafia as a way-station in the shipment of cocaine to the US. Marihuana, cocaine, and newer drugs like 'crack' are finding a growing market in the Dominican Republic. Casa Abierta opened its doors in 1974. It is an 'open house' not only because it provides walk-in treatment for young drug addicts, but also because its 18-person team

BELINDA COOTE

believes that the drug problem calls for society to find alternative solutions. "*Drug addiction is the symptom of a system of problems which are social,*" says Casilda, "*but it manifests in the individual.*" So, the Casa Abierta team focus mainly on preventive educational campaigns with community organizations.

"Drug addiction is the symptom of a system of problems which are social."

"The only way you can win your rights is on the streets, not in the kitchen."

Further to the west, in the slum districts of Santo Domingo, communities are trying to find alternatives to their problems. In one community of small box-like houses, a group of 30 people meet in a small dimly lit community clinic, trying to hear themselves talk over a torrent of noise from car horns, ghetto blasters and people shouting to each other in the street outside. The clinic is run by PROSAIN, the Project for Integrated Health. For three months the community has been without a pumped civic water supply. They have been relying instead on the private cowboy water trucks who charge exorbitant rates. PROSAIN estimated in 1987 that each truck was making over £1,500 profit each month. The community representatives debate what to do to get the water company to comply with its obligations and turn the water back on. *"The man from the water company should be locked up,"* says one woman to general laughter. An earnest young student, tired of the discussion between the women, harangues them: *"This is a fight. It is between rich and poor. We should strike. Tomorrow. No more talk. The only way you can win your rights is on the streets, not in the kitchen."* A woman interrupts, tired of being taught to suck eggs. *"Neither in the university,"* she retorts. The other women laugh. In the end they agree to canvas the support of more community organizations for a strike at the end of the month, closing down businesses and organizing marches to shame the authorities.

This small incident illustrates the fact that lack of medical services are only one of the health problems that poverty and powerlessness create. Accordingly PROSAIN's community clinics and the medical care they offer to the slum dwellers are only one part of their work. They also stress education with community groups, putting the health problems of the poor in a wider social context.

WOMEN IN
THE CARIBBEAN

4

Women, in many families, have to shoulder an unequal burden of the work. As in Jamaica's Hannah Town, many households are headed by women, who have to bear the burden of making a living alone for their children. In many rural areas, marriage is too expensive and cohabitation is common. In many cases, absentee fathers are reluctant to pay child-support. In the cane fields, women (who form one fifth of the labour force in the industry in Jamaica) do the most menial tasks for the lowest wages.

Christina, mother of seven children, has been weeding on the Bernard Lodge sugar estate in Jamaica for the last 30 years. Almost 12,000 women fieldworkers are employed on the island by the multi-million dollar sugar industry. Weeding and spreading fertilizer are carried out mainly by the women. They earn J$11 (about £1.30) an acre. The higher-paying jobs go to the men – reaping, planting, spraying and loading.

"We bear nuff a de burden and get the least pay."

"We bear nuff a de burden and get the least pay," Christina says to the nods of other members of the gang.

Many countries, including especially Jamaica and the Dominican Republic, have established Free Trade Zones in a bid to attract foreign investment. Companies such as garment manufacturers producing denim jeans for export to the USA

have been attracted to the Zones by tax holidays and, since unions are forbidden, low wage-bills. Many of the low-paid workers in these zones, are women, especially young women.

FIGHTING THE DOUBLE BURDEN

Most farming women in the Caribbean bear a double burden. Up in the mountains in the east of the Dominican Republic, the women of the small town of San José de Ocoa call it the double day. After back-breaking work in the fields picking coffee or looking after the house, the small domestic vegetable plot and the animals, wives are expected to bathe,

feed and water their husbands, look after the children and, if they haven't been at home during the day, clean the house as well. When they have paid field work, women get a fraction of the wages their husbands receive for the same job. To make matters worse, wages are often paid directly to the man of the household.

The Association for Women's Development in San José de Ocoa helps women understand and find a way around their problems and helps them earn the money and respect they deserve. Based in the town and run by a group of professional women, the Association caters for the needs of the small rural communities in the district. Many of the problems don't only affect women, like illiteracy which is currently running at about 80% or lack of health care facilities. But, because women have to take on most of the responsibilities of bringing up children, they play a key role in the development of the community.

The Association trains women from the town and surrounding rural communities in basic health and in ways to make a bit more money. It also holds monthly meetings attended by all the local peasant women's associations where problems can be shared and solved.

The village of El Naranjal in the San José de Ocoa region is typical of the work the Association fosters. It has helped set up a sewing and a bee-keeping project, so the women can earn a bit of extra cash. But more important than the money is the power the women have gained since they started supporting and helping each other. Carmen Abreu who works

THE CARIBBEAN: MAKING OUR OWN CHOICES

in the sewing cooperative put it like this:

"Before being organized life was much harder. Now we have much more protection. Before, our husbands had much more control over our time and now we have become community leaders and we tackle all the problems together."

And that means tackling problems faced by the whole community, not just those of the women. A few years ago the Dominican government declared that they were going to build an enormous dam to provide water for the capital city. To get to the dam they were also going to build a major road that would plough through the middle of El Naranjal, destroying the village.

With their new-found confidence and abilities to organise, the women of the village opposed the scheme. The protests they lead persuaded the government to re-route the road away from their village. This won them the respect of the men as Carmen explained:

"We've still got a long way to go. But now we've learnt to identify what our needs are and the needs of the community. Many women were very suspicious of organizing at first because we didn't realise how oppressed we were. Even when we knew we were not happy with our husbands they only had to help out one day in the kitchen and we would feel extremely lucky and grateful. And now our husbands are beginning to recognise the advantages of us being organized because we are bringing in extra money. There is still a lot of machismo [sexism]. But now the men can see what we can do, how we can organize for everybody's sake and that we can earn money and now they have got more respect for us."

Ironically, earning that respect and independence involves the women in even more work than the average "double day". Altagracia Haydee Castillo described her typical day:

"I get up at 6 am, wash and put the coal on the fire for the cooking while my husband is still sleeping. I put on the

*Women
often have
to shoulder
the whole
financial
burden of
childrearing.*

OXFAM PARTNER 3

CYNTHIA TAYLOR, 'HUCKSTER', DOMINICA

Roseau, capital of the tiny eastern Caribbean island of Dominica swarms with activity at the beginning of every week. Bananas and citrus fruit, trucked down from the slopes and upland valleys of the island's agricultural areas are unloaded, counted and packaged in the narrow lanes and streets. By late evening the rickety skiffs and ageing cargo boats in the harbour are deep-laden with crates and boxes of produce. Then aboard comes a procession of women who have spent the afternoon anxiously on the dockside, swearing furiously at every mistake of the loaders and crane operators with the fragile loads. These are the 'hucksters' of Dominica.

Small traders, they brave up to two days journey in these uncertain craft to sell the fruit in neighbouring islands of Guadeloupe, Antigua, Trinidad and Barbados. Collectively they make a significant contribution to the island's economy. In 1986 one ton of produce in every 50 exported was through the hucksters.

Cynthia Taylor is a huckster. Most hucksters, like her, are women, often from farming families. This reflects the traditional division of labour, where men do the farming and women do the marketing. Women often have to shoulder the whole financial burden of childrearing. Cynthia says: *"I have been in my trade over 20 years and I like it. I buy and I resell. That's what I'm doing for my living and to raise up my family. I have a large family. My husband is not employed. I can't depend on him for what we need. My husband does gardening. He plants his land. Then I sell what he produces to get what we need."*

The Dominica Hucksters Association, formed in 1981 and led by Cecil Joseph and Dora O'Garo, attempts to provide services and training to the hucksters. Today most of the island's 400 hucksters are members. This growth has not been easy. Each huckster is an independent entrepreneur, living off her wits to make an

ROSHINI KEMPADOO

eastern Caribbean dollar. She is a trader, buying directly from the farmers, a packager, a shipper and a marketer rolled into one. Competition and rivalry are strong. But times are changing and hucksters have to change with them if anyone is to gain.

The DHA managed to get a few members to keep accounts to see how bad the situation was. Few hucksters carry more than EC$2,000 worth of produce in one trip. The fare alone over to Guadeloupe is EC$200 and the boat owners overcharge for freight. On top of everything else, as much as 30% of the produce was getting damaged by being bruised or crushed in transit. *"Bagging the produce is no good. It's like you were throwing them away,"* says Cynthia. Many were actually losing money on each trip. So the hucksters began to see the value of banding together to get improved marketing regulations from the government, to negotiate lower freight costs from shippers, to operate a rotating loan fund. And one very simple concrete step – to use proper cartons (with start-up funding from Oxfam) to reduce damage to the produce. As Cynthia says: *"We couldn't deal with these problems as individuals. As a group we are stronger. We can get more attention."*

Through these activities, the huckster trade is changing. Cecil Joseph points to Cynthia and her daughter, Marjorie, as an example. Marjorie became a huckster as soon as she left school. On her first trip to Guadeloupe she sold 10,000 grapefruit. Cynthia has never handled that amount in her 20 years in the trade. Now Marjorie doesn't bother with the market place at all. She sells directly to the top hotels in Barbados. Informal traders are becoming formal exporters.

THE HUCKSTER SONG

Life can be so hard
Life can be so difficult
Struggling every day
Always far away
No rest, no sleep, no play
The traders are here to stay

I want you to listen to the story of the island trade
Where the work is so hard
They have to fight and struggle to make the grade
Buying, grading, clearing, crating, shipping
and selling, that is what they do
Moving through the Caribbean bringing good
food for me and you
From far, far away, the trade is with us each day

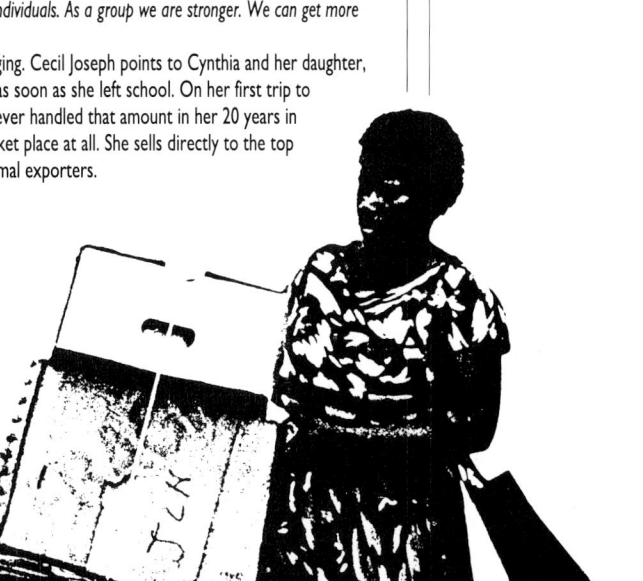

coffee and prepare breakfast for my husband and children. When they've all been fed, I start the four kilometre climb up into the mountains to pick coffee. While I'm working in the fields my daughters are doing the housework, putting on the beans to soak, washing the clothes, tending the hens, chickens, pigs, goats and the mule. I've got 11 children and seven are married but I've got enough daughters at home to help me.

"When I get back home at about 3 pm most of the housework has been done, so I wash and begin to prepare the supper. Then most evenings there's a meeting to go to – to talk about the bee-keeping project or the celebrations for our feast day. So often I won't get home until 10 o'clock at night and then I might have to do a bit of sewing or something before I go to bed. And my husband still complains that I'm lazy!

"On Thursdays I leave the fields an hour early and go and work on the bee-keeping project which the women's development association helped us set up."

The honey they sell through the bee-keeping project, helps bring in vital

extra cash. Altagracia can earn 24 pesos a day if she can collect her full quota of coffee. But that is only possible if she gets her children to help her. Without help she usually only earns 12 pesos. To feed her family Altagracia needs at least three pounds of rice a day – rice costs 2 pesos and 10 cents a pound. The large, green bananas called plantain, that also form a basic part of the diet, cost 70 cents each. Beans are the main source of protein and they cost five and a half pesos a pound, so before she's even paid for her eggs, oil, sugar and coffee, Altagracia has spent her wages. The money her husband earns as a small farmer helps pay for the rest.

Both Carmen and Altagracia are proud of what they have achieved so far, and are determined to keep on confronting the daily problems they are faced with.

Mercedes Jimenez, a social worker from the Association whose wages are paid by Oxfam, said: "We constantly get more and more demands from new communities which we can't ignore and we have tried to respond to all these, but our aim is to strengthen the current projects rather than form new ones. Eventually the older projects become self-sufficient and we can move on to new ones. But with major problems, like the appalling lack of health facilities and the very high illiteracy rates, we can only make a very small contribution."

CULTURE OF RESISTANCE

5

Development means more than earning a bit more money. It also means the capacity of poor people to analyze their problems and hopes, to express them, and to transmit them to others.

KEEPING ALIVE THE HOPES OF THE POOR

Song and poetry have always carried the message and hopes of the poor in the Caribbean. The topical Calypso songs of the English-speaking Caribbean are a kind of oral newspaper, spreading news and social comment through the islands. Often they deal with subjects that are embarrassing for the official media, such as the Barbadian calypso, Boots. Dealing with military spending, it was banned in 1983 by order of Tom Adams (the Tom of the song), the then Prime Minister.

Other forms, like *decima* in the Dominican Republic, and the performance poetry of the eastern

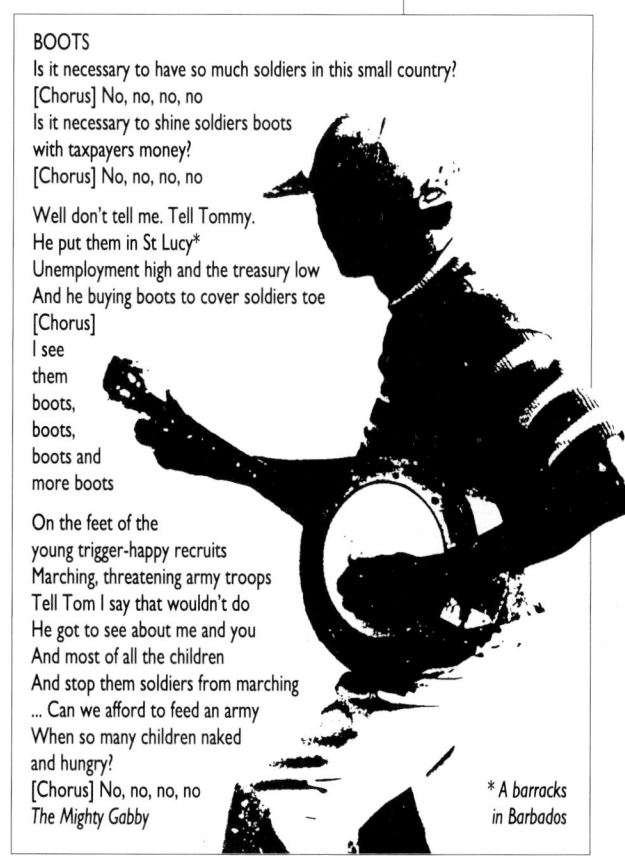

BOOTS
Is it necessary to have so much soldiers in this small country?
[Chorus] No, no, no, no
Is it necessary to shine soldiers boots
with taxpayers money?
[Chorus] No, no, no, no

Well don't tell me. Tell Tommy.
He put them in St Lucy*
Unemployment high and the treasury low
And he buying boots to cover soldiers toe
[Chorus]
I see
them
boots,
boots,
boots and
more boots

On the feet of the
young trigger-happy recruits
Marching, threatening army troops
Tell Tom I say that wouldn't do
He got to see about me and you
And most of all the children
And stop them soldiers from marching
... Can we afford to feed an army
When so many children naked
and hungry?
[Chorus] No, no, no, no
The Mighty Gabby

* A barracks
in Barbados

Caribbean, poetry for recitation, follow in this tradition.

> ... Mister, don' feel up de fish
> If you not buying, leave it!
> No Sir, sea egg price gone up.
> No Sir, I ain't put it up
> Is de government
> What you say sir?
> If you could take my picture?
> How much you paying?
> We natives doesn't pose
> For free again!
> Alright. But lemme
> Fix up face.
> All you move,
> Move darlin', move little bit darlin'
> (*Tim Tim*)

Oxfam supports cultural projects throughout the Caribbean. One example is the Movement for Cultural Awareness in Dominica, a group of writers, researchers, musicians and actors – six men and two women – which aims to preserve and develop national cultural forms which can foster cultural identity and provide people with techniques for expressing and analyzing their problems.

The MCA say: "*Folklore and the local Creole language [are] being used in a process of discovering more about people's concerns.*" They are determined, not only that the culture of Dominica should be Dominican, but that it should belong to everyone rather than to an elite of professional performers. Oxfam is supporting a new MCA programme to pass on their skills by training a core of grassroots cultural workers.

Sometimes the hopes of poor people are driven underground, expressed only secretly. When that happens, culture provides an all-important means of keeping hope alive. The occupation of Haiti by US marines during the early years of this century, for example, prompted Haitian intellectuals to search for their roots in African culture.

During the military occupation, there was a questioning and a re-examination of Haitian identity. It was

ROSHINI KEMPADOO

at this time that African cultural roots began to be recognized, researched and valued. From this came an explosion of cultural forms that was at once energetic and romantic. There were the 'naive' Haitian paintings that have become world-famous with their

"*The spiritual or cultural [is also] the subject of Development. When one speaks of raising the level of consciousness of a people, one means widening their sense of their own possibilities. It means giving them hope that action, purposeful action, can result in an advance over their existing state. Without hope thßere may be change, but it will hardly qualify as development.*"
Barry Chevanne,
University of the West Indies

colour, their vibrancy and their geometric patterning that share common roots with West African art. This cultural movement was an expression of Haitians' rejection of their foreign oppressors. But at the same time, this art betrays the myth-making of a generation of intellectuals in the 1920s and 1930s whose ardent nationalism still rested on a romantic and patronizing notion of the 'native', whose roots go back to the philosopher Rousseau and the painter Gaugin.

When the occupiers withdrew, the ultimate inheritor of the cultural renaissance, the self-questioning and the new nationalism was a diminutive shy black doctor and amateur anthropologist – Francois Duvalier. He won out in a three-way scramble for the presidency in 1957. He appealed to the masses as a black, by presenting himself as the triumph of the blacks over the mulatto elite, while skillfully appeasing, and at the same time controlling, the army and the business sector.

Under the terror imposed by the Duvalier dictatorship, culture again became important, as it had been under the marines. One Haitian observed:

"In our country, song has been one of the means most used by the peasants to

Song has been one of the means most used by the peasants to recount their joys, their disappoint-ments and their hopes.

recount their joys, their disappointments and their hopes, even though they are despised by exploiters of all colours. In the process of deterioration of our culture ... some animators are struggling to preserve these songs. Clotaire, a young peasant originally from the Central Plateau, captured the attention of many people with his songs of revolt, songs in which he questions an existence which is brutal and absurd – an existence which destroys physically and alienates mentally the peasant. Composer and singer Clotaire Alexandre raises his voice against this situation."

An example of efforts to preserve this popular culture was a week-long workshop held in 1982 by Clotaire, with over 30 peasants drawn from 'animation' (community development) groups in the region:

"The participants were so interested in learning the songs that they lost track of time. These songs which invite deep reflection were introduced by the composer and discussed by the participants. These members of [animation] groups, on their return to their communities, had the task of teaching others what they had learned.

THEATRE IN EDUCATION

"Me no haffi shame fe talk."

Theatre can be a powerful technique allowing communities to explore their problems. In Jamaica, the Sistren theatre group and the Groundwork Theatre Company do just this. Sistren's drama-in-education workshops are aimed at working women. Groundwork's programme focusses on youth who make up over 60% of Jamaica's population. More than a quarter of young people are without regular jobs.

Sistren, which means *"sisters"*, began in 1977, when ten unemployed women given temporary work as street cleaners on a government job creation scheme approached a director to help them put on a play.

> Every mother a working mother
> We inna it up to our neck.
> One lickle fall and we wreck

They explored their own suffering to put together their first play. Pauline Crawford, a founder member explains:

"We were invited to do a piece for the May workers' day. We asked the drama tutor for help in doing a drama piece on how women suffer. We did a piece on the struggle in a garment factory. It was well received. They said 'You should stick together'. This was the birth of Sistren. We wanted to become more professional. I wanted the play to show what forces caused my mother to treat me like that. This was how 'Belly Woman Bangarang' came about. Then we had to deal with the problems of our men at home and our children. You're learning the skills, preparing a production, and at the same time you have to look after your home life. There was a lot of energy among us women, but when you came home it was 'why you come home so late? where my dinner?'"

The Groundwork Theatre Company was founded in 1981 as an arm of the Jamaica School of Drama, but it failed to secure the government funding it had been promised and began to chart a new path. Moving closer to development work, it changed its original name – the Graduate Theatre Company – to reflect its new orientation.

They tour the island's secondary schools, using drama to help relate the English curriculum, with students' lives. There is a further spin-off as a member of the Company explained:

"For us, the far greater value is found in the connection which they [the students] make with the cultural forms which we use in the presence of their teachers ... [This] legitimises for them their cultural forms and allows them to recognise that there is value in what is theirs – their language, their songs, their rhythms, their movement – therefore encouraging recognition that there is value in themselves. Several students come to us after the sessions and say in one form or another 'I feel proud when I see you in my school'. 'Me no haffi shame fe talk'."

The community drama/animation programme takes this conclusion to its logical next stage: the use of drama to empower the participants. During 1987, for example, the programme focused on the coffee-farming community of Green Hill/Cascade Hills in Portland. Most of the estates are owned by Japanese firms, government farms or absentee landlords. The coffee estates provide employment but wages are low and services like running water or electricity are rare. GTC's work in the area, using drama as a means of exploring the community's problems with young people, led to the formation of the 30-strong Cascade Supersonic Action Club. They identified lack of health services as one of the community's main problems and worked up a play to dramatize health conditions to the community. *"At last we start to do something for we self,"* said one group member. In 1986, similar workshops in the community of Jericho in Hanover identified and then

Over the years Sistren have become more than skilled performers: they have also attempted to use theatre in community work.

ROSHINI KEMPADOO

BELINDA COOTE

overcame a feeling of hopelessness and led to the formation of the organization Jericho Survival Incorporated which focused on the lack of water supplies. The popular theatre programme now sustains eight community theatre groups in different parishes.

For Sistren too, professional theatre is not enough. They have become one of the best known popular theatre groups in the Caribbean. But over the years Sistren have become more than skilled performers: they have also attempted to use theatre in community work, as Pauline explained:

"We weren't satisfied that we were just doing professional theatre. There is one kind of theatre for upper class people. We didn't feel comfortable at all. We decided we wanted a more intimate kind of theatre where women could come together, laugh, cry, and just feel good about it. So we started the workshops. Sometimes dramatic pieces came out of them, because, often, Jamaican women can't tell you something without acting it out."

Sistren too have helped the growth of community drama groups. One of these is the cultural group of sugar workers on the Frome estate, where Sistren provided training in collaboration with the Social Action Centre (a Jamaican non-governmental organization) which stimulated the formation of the group.

The present day labour movement in Jamaica owes its origins to a strike in 1938 by workers on the Frome estate in Westmoreland, with women in the forefront, demanding better than the 3d and 6d a day they were paid. And it is particularly the women

THE CARIBBEAN: MAKING OUR OWN CHOICES

sugar workers who are making a contribution to keeping their heritage alive. The Sugar Workers Cultural Group was formed in 1980 by workers from ten farms on the Frome Estates at a time when the sugar estates were briefly turned into cooperatives under the Manley government. Through poems, songs and drama the predominantly female group communicated the experience of the sugar workers. Their performances speak to the workers in their own idiom about the problems of the area. Their activities provide one of the few channels for organization and expression for the 2,000 workers on the estates – more isolated from each other since the disbanding of the cooperatives in 1981.

One sugar worker said that the cultural group had given them more pride in themselves, showing them that they should *"not copy other people's culture but should look into our day to day work on the farms and at home and make use of them. This was our first experience in writing our own song, bringing out the fact that we are one of the best set of workers in the Jamaican society."*

THE CONTRADICTORY CARIBBEAN IDENTITY

Cultural identity is not a luxury. It is also a pressing need for a region searching for a united voice in the international game of trade and power pacts. From sugar and slavery, bananas and bauxite, to finance and free-trade zones: since 1492 the Caribbean's wealth has enriched others.

"There has always been an external view of this region that it has no internal view of itself. That is why you still think the first world war had something to do with you. But it had nothing to do with you except for using you as cannon fodder. There is a view that the region should become a series of service stations (for tourism, for banking and so on). We have to find the language to put our people in a critical relation to these things."
George Lamming, novelist, Barbados

For the Caribbean to negotiate a better deal for itself, it must first recognize itself as a region. Forging a common Caribbean purpose and identity has not been easy. Attempts at Caribbean unity, such as the short-lived Caribbean Federation (1958 - 1961) among the English-speaking territories failed, though a Caribbean Economic Community (CARICOM) was set up in 1973. The admission of Haiti and the Dominican Republic to

PETER LARSEN

the European Community's Lomé Convention has tripled the Caribbean population eligible for benefits under the scheme. This has been a source of some concern to English speaking Caribbean nations already members of the scheme. The Caribbean's identity is a contradictory one. It is a region with common problems but divided by barriers of language, of political and of cultural tradition. The English-speaking islands tend to be drawn into the cultural orbit of the UK or US; the French-speaking islands into that of France and so on. Even travel routes often link the islands to the United States rather than to each other. To fly from Kingston, Jamaica to Santo Domingo in the Dominican Republic may involve flying first over the Dominican Republic to US territory in Miami or Puerto Rico and then back again.

Though many factors pull the Caribbean islands apart, they share, at the same time, a common identity. It is an identity forged in common African descent and the suffering of slavery; an identity forged in a common culture of labour between the descendents of African slaves and Asian indentured workers.

Non-governmental organizations have perhaps gone further than governments in trying to share experiences and build links. Among those whom Oxfam has supported are CARIPEDA, a regional body of development organizations, the Puerto Rico-based Caribbean Project for Justice and Peace, and the Caribbean Conference of Churches (CCC). The CCC also helps to share ideas through a monthly newspaper *Caribbean Contact*, produced from Barbados . With a circulation of 28,000, the newspaper is, for many people, the main source of Caribbean-wide news seen through Caribbean eyes. Sometimes it is the only source. True to its name, it relies on a network of contacts throughout the islands. Though published mainly in English, it carries a few articles in Spanish and French.

CREOLE: THE POLITICS OF LANGUAGE

Even the language problem is not as difficult as it might seem. Haiti is often thought of as a French-speaking

DOMINIQUE LEBRUN, LITERACY WORKER, HAITI

Dominique Lebrun was part of the Misyon Alpha team. She explained: *"If you don't know how to read and write, you can't participate in local government. People know this is the way they can resolve their health problems, their irrigation problems, their credit problems – in short, their development problems."* Misyon Alpha was a huge undertaking, but the enthusiasm was tremendous.

In the winter months, the sun is already going down by 5.30 when the farmers come in from their fields. There is no electricity in most of the isolated villages. An oil lamp to light a literacy centre would cost almost a third of a year's income for an agricultural labourer, and more than the church can afford to provide. *"But,"* says Dominique, *"I have seen people come in with their own little alcohol lamps, costing about 30p, lighting the centres with a flicker of many tiny flames."*

The literacy programme worked in a multiplier fashion, training a group of 21 *educateurs*, who trained 250 *formateurs*, who in turn trained about 2,500 *moniteurs* at the base. The dedication of the *moniteurs* too was tremendous. Themselves poor people who earned only a token payment of around £1.60 a month for their work, they often set out to teach at 4.00 in the afternoon without having eaten a slice of bread all day. They might walk up to five miles to reach the literacy centres where they taught.

The campaign's pilot phase taught 7,000 people in 14 parishes between September 1985 and June 1986. The second phase lasted until the end of 1987 and reached some 75,000 of a planned 93,000 people, with around 50% of participants reaching full literacy. This is perhaps remarkable given Haiti's recent upheavals: the overthrow of the Duvalier regime in 1986 and the violence leading up to and accompanying elections in 1987 and early 1988. In the rapidly worsening situation leading up to two military coups in 1988, the project was suspended. However, many *moniteurs* are continuing the work as best they can in isolation, training more people in their own areas.

territory, while Dominica and St Lucia are English-speaking. The elites, who usually speak only these European languages, are not able to communicate directly with each other, or (increasingly) have all to speak English. But some groups of ordinary people have an alternative. They, in fact, share a common language: Creole. Though in the past it was described as 'pidgin' rather than a

true language, Creole is in fact a unique language created by the slaves, a mixture of African and European languages.

This has made it possible for groups from different parts of the Caribbean to get together and exchange experience. People from Dominica and St Lucia for example have been able to attend training courses in animation in Haiti run in Creole.

There have been growing moves towards recognizing Creole as an official language. Each year Dominica celebrates a day for Creole, with cultural events and radio broadcasts in the language. In Haiti, before the fall of Duvalier, 70% of radio broadcasts were in French and 30% in Creole. Now the reverse is true – 70% of broadcasts are in Creole and the new constitution recognizes the language – though in the current political uncertainty the status of that constitution remains ambiguous. French remains however the language of state business.

Creole and popular culture in Haiti were given a big impetus by a literacy campaign that ran briefly from 1985, just before the overthrow of the Duvalier dynasty, until the 1988 military coup. Run by the Catholic Church, Misyon Alpha aimed to make all Haitians literate in Creole, in a country where 80% of the people can neither

"Tourists to Haiti have habitually spent a few hours ashore, heard drumbeats from the hills and shuddered deliciously as they conjured up images of weird goings-on black-magic, licentious dances and frenetic orgies."
James Leyburn, The Haitian People, Yale University Press, 1966

read nor write. Drawing on popular cultural tradition, they called their method *"Taste Salt"*. Haitians say that zombies, the undead automata of voudou tradition, remain slaves until they taste salt; once they have tasted salt they become conscious and aware of their rights.

VOUDOU: THE POLITICS OF RELIGION

Nothing is more subterranean and more misunderstood in the Caribbean's African heritage than voudou, so beloved by Hollywood. In the hands of a hundred B-movie directors, it was transformed into a bestiary of evil and barbarism.

To understand voudou, says Haitian scholar Laennec Hurbon, you have to understand the way in which the West invented the concept of barbarism to justify its conquest and exploitation of the Third World through the dual concepts of *"barbarism/civilization"* (see *Le Barbare Imaginaire*). In reality, voudou emerged among the slaves in Haiti, as a culture which allowed them to confront and understand their domination. Like any other religion, it offers answers to the questions of life: of pain and joy, of purpose and meaning, of morality and health. The spirits of voudou have the power to alter the course of nature, to cure sickness sent by an enemy, to avert misfortunes and to foretell the future. It is a culture that owes much to African roots and keeps them alive in Haiti today. The slaves who were brought in chains from West Africa, and above all from Dahomey, brought with them their spirits, their dances

and their songs. Elements from different African cultures were forged together, with elements of Catholicism, to create voudou. The strongest voudou spirit of all is Le Bon Dieu, the Christian God, whose potency over the other spirits mirrors the power of the white slavemasters.

In the early years of the nineteenth century the slave rebellion was hatched in voudou circles. The priests or *houngans* were crucial community leaders. The drumming in the night, which the white planters thought of comfortably as mere dance rhythms, spread the plans from one community to another. Sorcery invoked the favour of the spirits for the rebellion.

Under the dictator Duvalier this connection between voudou and the aspirations of the poor was turned on its head. He usurped the symbolism of voudou as one element in his apparatus of terror. His dreaded *tonton macoute* (which means "bogeyman" in Creole) and a circle of prominent sorcerers became what one Haitian commentator described as *"the government of the night"*. But practitioners in voudou were also prominent in the opposition which overthrew Duvalier. The new constitution, written after the overthrow, brought voudou out of the shadows and recognized it as a national religion.

Voudou, an expression of the African roots of Haiti, this most African society in the Caribbean, has its echoes on other islands. The Pocomania and Rastafarianism of Jamaica also preserve African roots. The origins of the great Caribbean carnivals are in slave celebrations, a 'safety valve', when slaves became 'masters' for a day.

THE CARIBBEAN: MAKING OUR OWN CHOICES

RASTAFARIANISM

In the early decades of this century there was a stirring among colonized peoples of national and ethnic consciousness. The Caribbean was no exception. Jamaica's Marcus Garvey prompted an international stirring of black consciousness. Rastafarianism found its origins in this stirring. The Rastafarians, poor farmers in the main, took their name from Ras Tafari, Emperor Haile Sellasie of Ethiopia, a major African nation not then under direct colonial control. For the emerging Rastafarian religion, it represented a spiritual alternative to the European-dominated world. The

HERB & SPICE PRODUCTION, DOMINICA

Blow's Agro Productions is a group of eight Rastafarians (seven men and one woman) in the Eastern Caribbean island of Dominica. Rastafarians have had a notoriously hard time in the island, and Blow's provides the group with a living, selling herbs and spices. This has enabled them to preserve their cultural identity.

The group started with a fruit and vegetable stall in the centre of the island's capital, Roseau. Other activities of their group were basket crafts and T-shirt printing. They expanded into the collection, curing, grinding and packaging of herbs and spices such as peppermint, basil, cinnamon, bayleaves and ginger. Government laboratories helped them with grinding and heat-sealing of packages.

Oxfam helped with part of the cost of buying and freighting from the UK a tea-bagging machine.

Blow's say that the project is "helping to stabilize a forward moving roots movement, for as brothers and sisters from the heart of the ghetto, any progress achieved marks a liberation progression, in that means become available for other socio-cultural activities." They expect that their operation could extend to 15-20 people. They have found a ready market for their product in the King George Street grocery shop and could expand to other shops, supermarkets, hotels and prisons. Moreover, they have contacts with the French Antilles and envisage marketing through Martinique in the medium term.

ROSHINI KEMPADOO

THE CARIBBEAN: MAKING OUR OWN CHOICES

world of the white empires they called *"Babylon"* to them meant sin, suffering and exploitation. Ethiopia held out the symbolic promise of an African homeland for Africans. At times persecuted, the Rastafarian community, remains today a strong assertion of black and African identity.

THE RIGHT TO PRESERVE CULTURE: ANIMATION THROUGH ART

Today there is a new need to reaffirm Caribbean culture.

Foreign radio and TV programmes by satellite from the USA add to historical separation, so that people on the smaller islands may often know more about fashion, politics and social life in the USA than they do about the next island.

"What is taking place quietly in the living rooms of thousands of Caribbean family units as they sit innocently before their television sets frightens us. It is a process of de-culturization which is painless but also very thorough and long-lasting."

So says the Caribbean Publishing and Broadcasting Association about the effects of US television programmes on Caribbean people. About three quarters of all programmes shown on Caribbean TV are foreign, mainly from the US. The Association fears that dependence on US TV will become so strong that external cultural values will displace national ones.

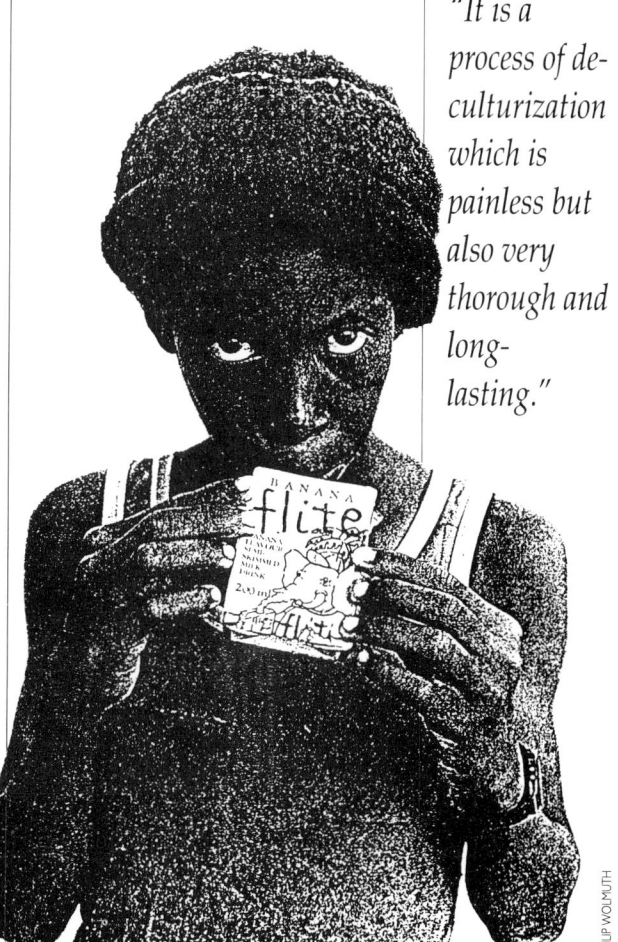

PHILIP WOLMUTH

"It is a process of de-culturization which is painless but also very thorough and long-lasting."

Night in Roseau, capital of Dominica. The shrill chirruping of the cicadas begins. The grid of streets and clapboard houses that runs down to the waterfront is dark. The sound of waves lapping on the shore is restful. Everywhere is the smell of food cooking. People are hanging out in the streets: a young couple in the shadow of a doorway; a group of youths at a pavement table playing dominoes, laughing as they slap the chips down. Down by the harbourside market, empty now for the night, a television set blares out from one of the small houses. Moths and insects swirl in the shafts of the TV's blue light that ray out eerily between the wooden slats of the wall. An American announcer's voice urges viewers to buy Alka Seltzer. A man rocks on the porch looking into the house at the TV inside. At the roadside a youth leans across the roof of a parked car, looking in at the TV too.

OXFAM PARTNER **5**

NEIL MacDONALD

ROXANNA RAMIREZ, MUSICIAN, LA ROMANA, DOMINICAN REPUBLIC

"You hear a lot of American music here," says Roxanna Ramirez. *"It's popular. Young people dance to it. But this is
not our music. This is not the way we move our bodies. Wherever we go we see young people dancing in the US style,
mixing our language with theirs, behaving like North Americans, using drugs, assuming this to be good because it is
what they see on films, TV etc and not as what it really is: the systematic replacement of values of this nation by those
of another."*

Roxanna looks at the replica Coliseum in the Casa del Campo tourist complex. International stars like
Frank Sinatra and Julio Iglesias helicopter in here to entertain the tourists. Workmen are readying it for
another glittering musical evening. Behind her, North American and European tourists shop for imported soft
drinks and breakfast cereals. *"Not even the stone is Dominican,"* says Roxanna. *"They decided to build a Roman
city for the tourists, and they imported the stone from Italy."*

Casa del Campo lies in La Romana province in the
south of the Dominican Republic. It was built by the
Gulf and Western Company on Gulf and Western
land. The gates to the exclusive complex are
patrolled by Gulf and Western security men. Until
recently the US multinational company owned 2% of
the entire country. They built the world's largest
sugar refinery here, in the midst of acre after acre of
Gulf and Western sugar cane. La Romana, the third
largest province in the country, is almost a state
within a state.

Roxanna was one of nine women who, in 1979,
started a cultural group called Esclavas del Fogón –
Slaves of the Stove. Today, in the poor communities

of La Romana, they nurture eight amateur groups with 200 members. Oxfam has supported them since 1985. *"We are searching for what we are, for what we are losing,"* Roxanna explains. *"Our fundamental aim is to rescue our home grown culture and return it to the communities. For instance, we have many musical forms here which reflect our African heritage – chuines for example is a traditional form from the countryside. It takes the form of an improvised lament with a group response. People use it to express their reality – their calamities, their sadness, how hard it is to be a peasant and work so many hours and gain so little. It can be about any theme – love or inflation, or the problem of not having clean drinking water. Then we have other forms like salvé for dancing."*

PHILIP WOLMUTH

The Slaves have nurtured eight cultural groups in poor communities around La Romana. Their 200 members use street theatre, dance, music and poetry to interpret their own lives and problems. Many of them are underemployed, selling whatever they can in the streets, or taking odd jobs. Still others work in La Romana's Free Trade Zone, where low wages attract foreign companies to set up *"screwdriver plants"*, assembling electronic components or making up garments for re-export to the rich countries.

The shanty town of Rio Salado is one such community. Roxanna and the other Slaves clearly feel more at home in its rutted earthen alleyways and flimsy timber houses than in Casa del Campo. The heat is blistering. People hang out of their windows to catch a breath of air. The alleyways sloping steeply down to the filthy river are running sewers in the dry season and torrents of mud when the rains come. In the river, where the water froths with sewage and industrial waste, a group of young men are diving off the rocks. People call out *"Hey slaves, how's it going?"* A young girl calls shyly from her window. *"Hi little slave,"* calls back Roxanna.

The Slaves are part of this community, loved and respected. In contrast to the generally dilapidated air of the community is the small concrete-walled park with plants, shady trees and benches. *"Before, there was nowhere here for people to rest,"* said one resident. *"Then the Slaves got the local government to put up some money, and they put in some money from their performances, and we got this park."*

"Culture is not something separate from everyday life. We deal with general problems," says Roxanna. *"Like how to get enough to eat, lack of schooling, lack of clean water. That is why we have support. Because culture can only be rescued, can only come alive, when it is connected with the struggle of life, when it is an instrument of struggle. As well as allowing people to educate themselves,"* says Roxanna, *"we want them to enjoy themselves. We are not pamphleteers. We want them to laugh and dance."*

> *"Culture can only be rescued, can only come alive, when it is connected with the struggle of life."*

"There is nothing, repeat nothing, to harvest."

LESLEY ROBERTS

THE CARIBBEAN: MAKING OUR OWN CHOICES

DISASTERS – RESOURCEFULNESS AND COOPERATION

6

Caribbean people need to be resourceful. Along with all the other problems they have to cope with, there is the ever-present worry of natural disaster. The Caribbean is a hurricane-prone area. Between June and November each year, farmers anxiously monitor the course and progress of the 30-60 tropical storms any one of which could develop into a hurricane and wreak havoc with homes and crops, especially the fragile banana and plantain trees. In September 1988 Hurricane Gilbert, the worst tropical storm in the Caribbean this century, devastated much of Jamaica and the south coast of Haiti in a 2,500 mile sweep of destruction across 15 countries of the Caribbean, Mexico and Central America. Over 500 people were killed and over a million lost their homes.

A Jamaican development worker said immediately after Gilbert struck: *"The storm destroyed everything we have built up in decades – crops, homes, schools, hospitals."* Almost one in four Jamaicans were made homeless and, in some areas up to 100% of the island's vital banana, coffee and coconut crops were felled. The hurricane left a landscape of battered and uprooted vegetation, overflowing streams and damaged telephone and electric cables. A member of Oxfam staff reported: *"there is nothing, repeat nothing, to harvest."* In one area near Portland only one building was left standing – the school – which was filled with children. All the adults appeared to have been washed out to sea.

Jamaica is still rebuilding its economy. A member of Oxfam staff paid tribute to the spirit of the people, starting from the first days after the storm, saying: *"it's really impressive the way people are working together and helping each other."* Despite the destruction, natural disasters can also bring out the best in people, as Noreen John of the Dominica-based Small Projects Assistance Team explained:

"[The hurricane of 1979] really

"The storm destroyed everything we have built up in decades – crops, homes, schools, hospitals."

brought out the vulnerability of the economy. The whole banana crop was destroyed. There was no electricity – it took us two years before it was restored in my community. Food was scarce – there was only fresh fish to eat. People had to go back to the resourcefulness of the old days – to the way the Caribs and the African slaves preserved food, such as smoking meat. It brought out the resourcefulness and the cooperative spirit. It has been ignored for a long time. But then people helped each other. We had to get back together. Perhaps that is a lesson in itself."

In nearby St Vincent, these lessons have been learned too.

"There was this man. He was sheltering under a tree with his animals. He bent down to stretch his legs. When he stood up to lean back against the tree – tree gone!" Earlene Horne, General Secretary of the National Farmers Union (see page 6), laughs as she tells the story of Hurricane Emily. She was on-site to inspect relief efforts in the Mamiaqui valley on the east of the small Caribbean island. Hurricane Emily that tore away that tree in September 1987, also devastated in 15 minutes 35-40% of the banana trees on which the island's economy depends. The government estimated that the storm damaged around 200 homes.

In 1987, Vincentians were already reeling under the impact of three disasters in 12 months. In 1986, Hurricane Danielle destroyed 60-65% of the banana crop. Then in the summer of 1987, just before Emily struck, a severe drought throughout the eastern Caribbean shrivelled the fruit and brought a 40% drop in earnings.

The NFU organized mutual-aid work teams in the valley to clear fallen trees and replant the young banana shoots. Oxfam helped with a grant. Earlene explained the basis of the work-teams as she set a punishing pace through the debris on the muddy hillsides. *"The teams help people who're not in the union too, as long as they contribute their labour too to help others. Of course, people who can't work, like old people, don't have to participate."* Three weeks after the storm, thanks to the rapid mobilization of the 10 teams, the work was largely complete. The NFU, together with other Vincentian organizations, also helped to repair 40 damaged houses. Every large vehicle making its way up the winding hill roads, was pressed into service. Even the brightly-painted island buses were bulging not only with their usual loads of passengers but also with timber and corrugated iron sheeting for roof repairs.

CONCLUSION

7

The Small Projects Assistance Team grew out of a hurricane. SPAT founder member Joey Peltier perhaps speaks for much of the grassroots development experience in the Caribbean, when he explains how the group was formed in 1981:

"When it became apparent that relief was not the answer. We had to develop tools for self-reliance. The main problem was building confidence. This is a general problem in the West Indies – the legacy of slavery – a lack of self-esteem and assertion of rights. When we started working with people, they were afraid even to put their hands up in meetings. Now they have become community leaders and spokespersons. Some have even been elected to local office. If you're able to work with people from the bottom up, in building leadership in communities, in health groups, sports associations, village associations, you're laying the foundations for people to make their own choices."

This has been an important lesson for Oxfam to learn in two decades of support for development in the Caribbean. Relief remains necessary when natural disaster hits. But relief is not enough. Nor can the problems of poverty be addressed by simply throwing money at them. We have learned that if people are to make progress, they must participate in shaping their own destinies. And so, running through most of the work we support is a stress on the importance of supporting democratic groups of farmers, workers, communities, women and youth. Within this we have learned that there are special issues that need attention – the relationship between men and women, and the need to respect and enhance local cultural values.

As we have seen, a key priority of the Caribbean people we work alongside is a solution to the crisis of agriculture. In a region which is primarily agricultural, the Caribbean nevertheless has to import much of its basic food. Problems of landlessness, combined with the use of land for growing export crops have created extreme poverty in some rural areas

"... you're laying the foundations for people to make their own choices."

*Bringing
groups
together
across the
Caribbean
allows
people to
learn from
each other
and forge a
new sense of
unity.*

and are a basic cause of migration from the countryside to the cities, or even out of the Caribbean. For this reason farmers' groups are searching for new strategies to control and diversify their production.

A second priority is to help processes of networking. The divisions that exist within the Caribbean are the heritage of colonialism. Bringing groups together across the Caribbean allows people to learn from each other and forge a new sense of unity. And linking is important beyond the Caribbean too. Caribbean communities around the world, especially in the UK and North America have a great role to play. The solidarity, as well as donations, of people, black and white, in the UK and Ireland is a part of the partnership that Oxfam aims to foster.

WHAT YOU CAN DO

8

f you would like to support the struggle of people in the Caribbean for a better future, why not:

● Organize an exhibition on the Caribbean in your local library, school, church or town hall.
● Arrange a meeting on the Caribbean in your area. Oxfam can supply speakers, sometimes people who are visiting from the Caribbean itself.
● Make a donation to Oxfam's work to help communities in the Caribbean.

OXFAM CAN HELP YOU

EDUCATION:
If you are a teacher or belong to an educational group, Oxfam's Education programme and its local education workers around the country can help you teach about development issues. Oxfam produces education materials, audio-visual resources and simulation games which could help you. Contact: Oxfam Education Dept., at our national headquarters (address below).

CAMPAIGNS:
As you have seen, community groups throughout the Caribbean are campaigning for their rights. Oxfam's 'Hungry for Change' campaign in the UK and Ireland provides support by campaigning here on issues which can alleviate poverty overseas. 'Hungry for Change' groups are made up of volunteers who try to influence decision makers in their towns, such as MPs and Euro-MPs to implement juster trade policies, provide better overseas aid, soften the impact of debt repayments and much more. Please join a 'Hungry for Change' group and contribute to the process of change. Our partners overseas are asking us to take up the challenge – will *you*? For details of your nearest group contact your local Oxfam area office or national headquarters (see below).

RESOURCES:
Oxfam has many publications, videos, slide sets and leaflets which can tell you more about the way we work alongside over 2000 community groups in over 70 countries around the world. These can be bought or borrowed from Oxfam Area Offices around the country. You'll find your nearest one in the telephone directory, or phone our headquarters at 274 Banbury Road, Oxford OX2 7DZ (0865-56777).

SUGGESTED FURTHER READING

GENERAL

Catherine Sunshine, *The Caribbean: Survival, Struggle and Sovereignty.* EPICA, Washington DC, 1988.

Clive Thomas, *The Poor and the Powerless: Economic Policy and Change in the Caribbean.* Latin America Bureau, 1988.

Eric Williams, *From Columbus to Castro: The History of the Caribbean 1492-1969.* Andre Deutsch, London, 1970.

Pat Ellis (ed.), *Women of the Caribbean.* Zed Press, London, 1987.

JAMAICA

Belinda Coote, *The Hunger Crop: Poverty and the Sugar Industry.* Oxfam, Oxford, 1987.

Anthony Payne, *Politics in Jamaica.* C Hurst & Co, London, 1988.

HAITI

James Ferguson, *Papa Doc, Baby Doc: Haiti and the Duvaliers.* Basil Blackwell, Oxford, 1988.

David Nicholls, *From Dessalines to Duvalier: Race, Colour and National Independence in Haiti.* Macmillan, Basingstoke, 1988.

DOMINICAN REPUBLIC

Jan Knippers Black, *The Dominican Republic: Politics and Development in an Unsovereign State.* Allen & Unwin, London, 1986.

Roger Plant, *Sugar and Modern Slavery: A Tale of Two Countries.* Zed Press, London, 1987.

EASTERN CARIBBEAN

Robert Thomson, *Green Gold: Bananas and Dependency in the Eastern Caribbean.* Latin America Bureau, London, 1987.

A POTTED HISTORY

9

HAITI

Haiti occupies the western part of the island of Hispaniola. It is the poorest country in the Western hemisphere. Just over three quarters of the people live on the land. The official minimum wage is less than £1 a day and unemployment, according to the government, is at least 70%. Colonized by the French in 1697, Haiti was, in 1804, the first black colony to successfully fight for its political independence. The ex-slaves defeated Napoleon's armies and for more than 20 years occupied the Dominican Republic, uniting Hispaniola. Yet Haiti was unable to chart an independent course of economic development for itself. The colonial estates were largely dismantled and parcelled out. But subsequent division and redivision of land has created tiny plots hardly large enough to sustain life. At the same time, a local mullato elite emerged that concentrated wealth and power in its hands: today 1% of the population owns 60% of the land. France's other main Caribbean possessions, Guadeloupe and Martinique, remained in French hands and are external departments of France to this day.

Haiti became strategically significant for US trade routes after the building of the Panama canal. The country was under US military rule from 1915 to 1934. Francois Duvalier ('Papa Doc') ruled from 1957, when he came to power with the blessing of the US-trained army, until his death in 1971. Through his secret police force, the dreaded *tonton macoutes*, he made the island a by-word for poverty and repression. Human rights violations led the US to cut off military aid from 1962 to 1970. In the 1970s Haiti began to take a slightly different course under Jean Claude Duvalier who had succeeded his father in 1971. 'Baby Doc' Duvalier was closer to the US government and to the sector of the local elite which wanted to modernize the country. US companies had gained control of four out of five of Haiti's main exports – sugar, bauxite, sisal and light manufacturing: only coffee is locally owned. Between 1970 and 1976 US companies, attracted by cheap labour in Haiti, had installed 230 new industrial plants in the country. Companies which had moved from the US to Puerto Rico found the 'cost advantages' of Haiti unbeatable. Assembly of clothing from textiles produced in the US for re-export to the US is the largest component of the light manufacturing sector. Second to this comes the sewing of baseballs. Third is the electronic assembly industry.

However all of this failed to modernize a country in which the majority of the big landowners remained resistant to change and in which an estimated 20-40% of government income went directly into the Duvalier family coffers. In 1986 popular mobilizations prompted the US to withdraw support from the Duvalier regime and the dictatorship fell. The short-lived period of movement toward democracy was aborted when violence caused the cancellation of elections in November 1987. The military seized power again in 1988 through two coups.

DOMINICAN REPUBLIC, CUBA, PUERTO RICO AND THE SPANISH CARIBBEAN

The Dominican Republic occupies the eastern part of the island of Hispaniola. It was the first capital of Spanish America. Christopher Columbus personally led the first military campaign to subdue the native peoples of the island. But this did not lead to colonies on the English or French pattern. The Spanish *conquistadors* had no interest in developing a plantation economy. Hernán Cortes, conqueror of Mexico, refused a royal land grant saying: *"But I came to get gold, not to till the soil like a peasant"*. Only after the abolitions of slavery in Britain and France did sugar plantations develop on any large scale in the Spanish Caribbean, especially in Cuba. And by that time, Spain's power was already faltering. The United States, the new rising power in the region, moved in to occupy the vacuum, its companies securing controlling interests in the sugar plantations.

Spain finally relinquished control of the Dominican Republic in 1844, but the country fell under the sway of a succession of tyrants until in 1916 the United States took over, militarily occupying the country until 1924. In a pattern common throughout the Caribbean basin, they built up an armed force, the National Guard, and left a strong-man Rafael Trujillo at its head before they went home. In 1930 Trujillo seized power, beginning a dictatorial rule that was to last 31 years.

The Trujillo era ended with his assassination in 1961. He had been lining his own pocket too energetically: he was said to control a staggering 65-85% of the economy. The Dominican economic elite had had enough and threw him to the wolves. But his successor, the moderate nationalist Juan Bosch, who was elected president in 1962, went further than the elite wanted. Bosch refused to denationalize Trujillo's holdings, which had passed to the state on the dictator's death,and sought to limit the power of landowners and of foreign companies, while defending the rights of the peasants. Coup and counter-coup followed. The country was on the brink of revolution when 20,400 US marines went in in 1965. When elections were held again in 1966, Trujillo's ex-Vice President Joaquin Balaguer was the victor. Massive US investment, both government and private, followed. US companies gained control of most of the country's bauxite, sugar, nickel and gold. Of these, Gulf & Western took the lion's share, its sugar and other agro-industry interests covering 2% of the national territory, in a country where only 14% of the land surface is cultivable. The company also diversified into tourism and set up the first free trade zone on the island. More have been set up since, especially employing female labour at low wages in assembly plants for export. Balaguer lost the presidency in 1978 to the Dominican Revolutionary Party (PRD) for two terms of office. An octogenerian, Balaguer was re-elected in 1986.

The early history of Cuban independence also involved a period of US occupation. An independence movement was on the verge of ousting the Spanish in 1898 when US marines joined in on the side of the rebels in the Spanish-American war. This unnecessary help secured a strong influence for US interests in Cuban affairs. This influence was underscored during a period of national turmoil in 1917. US marines took over the island and ran it until 1923. For most of the period between 1925 and 1959 Cuba was ruled by two military strongmen: Gerardo Machado, nicknamed 'the Butcher', and then Fulgencia Batista. Batista's rule, in two separate periods after 1934, was characterized by such corruption and repression that Cuba became known as the *"whorehouse of the Caribbean"*. He was overthrown after 25 years by the revolution led by Fidel Castro.

The 1959 revolution in Cuba was an earthshattering event both in the Caribbean and more widely in Latin America. Though initially pledged to a mixed economy and elections in 1961, US hostility and suspicion that the revolution was communist became a self-fulfilling prophecy. Trade restrictions drove the island towards the eastern bloc for aid and trade. In 1961 came the abortive Bay of Pigs invasion by right-wing Cuban exiles, supported by the CIA. In 1962 came the Cuban missile crisis as the USSR backed down in the face of US military pressure and withdrew missiles it had stationed on the island in return for a US promise not to invade the island.

Puerto Rico, wrested directly from Spain in the Spanish-American war, became an associated territory of the United States, a status described by the United Nations decolonization committee as akin to a colony. Puerto Rico's status is to be the subject of a future referendum on the island. After the second world war, the territory became a show-case for the US-sponsored model of development in the Caribbean: the promotion of foreign export-oriented investment in what was called *"Operation Bootstrap"*.

JAMAICA AND THE COMMONWEALTH CARIBBEAN

Jamaica is the largest of the Commonwealth Caribbean islands. It was first colonized in 1509 by the Spanish, who wiped out the native Arawak inhabitants. Britain seized the island in 1655. Jamaica became one apex of the notorious and immensely profitable *"triangular trade"* carried on by the British merchant fleet: ships voyaged to Africa where they exchanged British manufactures for slaves; the slaves were sold to sugar plantation owners in Jamaica and the ships loaded with sugar for the voyage home. When slavery was abolished in the Caribbean in 1833, the plantation owners tried to force the ex-slaves to continue working for them by throwing them off the land they had previously been allowed to farm. But many ex-slaves simply moved onto lands owned by the Crown or by missionaries. This was the birth of a class of independent peasant farmers. The churches, which had helped the farmers get land, retain to this day a strong influence in these communities. In many of the territories, Trinidad and Guyana particularly, a further dimension is added to the racial mix by the descendents of labourers from the Indian subcontinent who were brought in to replace slave labour. Relationships between blacks and Asians have played an important, and at times troubled, political role in these countries.

Church-sponsored education programmes also created a stratum of articulate black middle class leaders. Marcus Garvey, forerunner of black consciousness and nationalism among poor Jamaicans, created the first modern political party in the 1920s and 1930s. He pressed for a wide range of social reforms including mass education, land reform, social welfare, trade union rights and self government. A general strike in 1938 marked the emergence into maturity of the modern Jamaican labour movement. Afterwards trade unionism was recognized and limited self-government and adult suffrage conferred by Britain. The island's two traditional parties, the Jamaica Labour Party and the Peoples National Party, have their origins also in the 1938 strike. The other territories went through broadly similar histories.

The old European empires began to dissolve after the second world war. Under the patronage of the United States, a new world trade order was being born, and this had its reflection in the Caribbean. Until the 1950s, over half Jamaica's trade was with Britain and 50% of its export earnings came from sugar. By the mid-1970s over half its exports went to the US and 46% of its export earnings came from bauxite. The short-lived Caribbean Federation of 1958-1961 was intended to be the political framework within which the British Caribbean colonies would achieve their independence. But the externally-imposed Federation was rejected by the Caribbean peoples and collapsed. The islands instead received their political independence of Britain piecemeal: Jamaica and Trinidad in 1962, Barbados and Guyana in 1966, with the smaller islands of the eastern Caribbean following (though a few have chosen to remain British dependencies). However, there have been moves since towards greater Caribbean integration. CARICOM, the Caribbean Community and Common Market was established in 1973. In the 1980s there was a return to the idea of federation again in the eastern Caribbean. Growing cooperation on security, with aid from the US and UK, has led on to idea of unity. There is however considerable antagonism to the proposal from a coalition of opposition parties, who argue that it will provide a basis for increasing US penetration of the region.

INDEX

Africa 2, 38, 53
Agriculture 4, 8–10, 47
  cane cutters 3, 34
  creole pig, Haiti 10
  decline in export-led development 8
  exports 8
  food imports 10
  grain silos 18
  Hillside Farmers' Association, Jamaica 3
  land hunger 3, 9
  mutual-aid groups, Haiti 18, 19
  mutual-aid groups, St Vincent 46
  mutual-groups, Dominican Republic 11
  National Farmers' Union, St Vincent 6, 46
  Nucleus of Coffee Producers, Dominican Republic 11
  single-crop economies 5, 8
  tool banks, Haiti 18
Alternative marketing
  Blow's Agro Productions, Dominica 40
  Haiti 18
  Hucksters Association, Dominica 26
  Nucleus of Coffee Producers, Dominican Republic 11
Animation 17–20, 32, 33, 38, 41

Bahamas 1, 9

Caribbean unity 35
Christopher Columbus 1
Churches
  Caribbean Conference of Churches 36
  Catholic Church, Haiti 39
  Hannah Town United Church, Jamaica 20
Colonialism 3
  independence 4
Commodities
  bananas 5, 6, 8, 13, 46
  bauxite 3, 5, 8, 10, 13
  coffee 11
  oil and asphalt 5, 8
  rum 8
  single European market 8
  sugar 3, 5, 8, 13, 23, 35, 42
Commodities: alternative marketing
  Nucleus of Coffee Farmers' Associations, Dominican
  Republic 11

Culture
  and development 30
  calypso 29
  Creole language 9, 36
  decima, Dominican Republic 29
  Groundwork Theatre Company, Jamaica 32
  performance poetry, eastern Caribbean 29
  Sistren, Jamaica 32
  Slaves of the Stove. Dominican Republic 42
  song workshops, Haiti 31
  Sugar Workers' Cultural Group, Frome Estates,
  Jamaica 35
  US influence 41, 42

Debt 15
Disasters
  Hurricane Danielle 46
  Hurricane David 11
  Hurricane Emily 46
  Hurricane Gilbert 21, 45
Dominica 6–8, 26, 30, 37, 38, 40, 41, 45
Dominican Republic 4, 8–11, 17, 21, 24, 29, 35, 36, 42,
51, 52
Drug addiction 21
Duvalier 31, 37–39, 51, 52

Eastern Caribbean 1, 5, 8, 13, 26, 27, 40, 46, 54
Education
  literacy, Haiti 38
Environment
  declining yields, Haiti 9
  erosion, Haiti 12
  pollution in banana industry 7
  reforestation 12
Export 5, 8, 10–12, 14, 15, 24, 47, 52–54
Export industries
  electronic components, Dominican Republic 42
  garment manufacturing, Dominican Republic 42
Export-earnings
  and development models 8, 10

Foreign influence
  culture 42
  US military actions 4, 30
Free trade zone 10, 24, 42

Grenada 4, 10, 13
Guadeloupe 4, 7, 26, 27, 51
Guyana 5, 8, 10, 13, 54

Haiti 4, 8–10, 16, 17, 19, 30, 35–39, 45, 51, 52
Health
  PROSAIN, Dominican Republic 22
Housing conditions 20, 22, 43

Income generation
  Dominica 40
  Hannah Town, Jamaica 21
Indentured labour 4
Indigenous peoples
  Tainu, Arawaks, Caribs 1

Jamaica 1, 3, 5, 8–10, 12, 13, 16, 20, 23, 24, 32, 34, 36, 39, 40, 45, 53, 54

Labourers
  cane cutters 3

Martinique 4, 12, 40, 51
Media
  Caribbean Contact 36
  foreign radio and TV 41
Migration 14
Multinational companies
  Alcan and Alcoa 8
  Alcoa 3
  and nationalization, Guyana and Jamaica 13
  fruit companies 6
  Gulf & Western 42
  Tate and Lyle 3

Pocomania 39
Projects supported by Oxfam
  Association for Women's Development, Dominican Republic 24
  Blow's Agro Productions, Dominica 40
  Caribbean Conference of Churches 36
  Caribbean Project for Justice and Peace 36
  CARIPEDA 36
  Casa Abierta, Dominican Republic 21
  DCCH, Haiti 12
  GRD, Haiti 18
  Groundwork Theatre Company, Jamaica 32
  Hillside Farmers' Association, Jamaica 3
  Hucksters' Association, Dominica 26
  IDEA, Haiti 17, 18
  Mel Nathan Institute, Jamaica 21
  Misyon Alpha, Haiti 37

National Association of Haitian Agronomists 12
National Farmers' Union, St Vincent 6
Papaye, Haiti 18
Projects for People, Jamaica 3
PROSAIN, Dominican Republic 22
Sistren, Jamaica 32
Slaves of the Stove, Dominican Republic 42
small coffee producers, Dominican Republic 11
Small Projects Assistance Team, Dominica 45, 47
song workshops, Haiti 31
St Lucia/Haiti exchange 38
Puerto Rico 4, 7, 36, 52, 53

Rastafarianism 39, 40

Slavery 2, 5, 38
  abolition of 4
St Lucia 29, 37, 38
St Vincent 6, 8, 46

Tourism 9, 13, 38, 42
Training
  animation centres, Haiti 18
  cultural workers, Dominica 30
  exchange visit: St Lucia/Haiti 38
  Hannah Town, Jamaica 21
  literacy workers, Haiti 37
  pig rearing, Haiti 12
  reafforestation, Haiti 12
  small coffee producers, Dominican Republic 11
Trinidad 5, 8, 10, 16, 26, 54

Urban poverty
  Hannah Town, Jamaica 20
  Rio Salado, Dominican Republic 42
  Santo Domingo 21, 22

Voudou 9, 38

Windward islands 6
Women
  cane cutters 23, 34
  heads of household, Jamaica 20
  heads of households 23
  hucksters, Dominica 26
  in free trade zones 24
  Slaves of the Stove, Dominican Republic 42

Youth
  Groundwork Theatre Company, Jamaica 33
  street children, Dominican Republic 21
  youth gangs, Jamaica 20